Eat More
DIRT

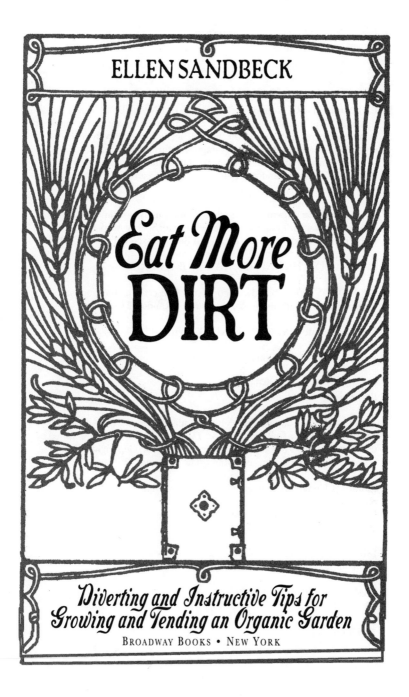

ELLEN SANDBECK

Eat More DIRT

Diverting and Instructive Tips for
Growing and Tending an Organic Garden

BROADWAY BOOKS • NEW YORK

BROADWAY

Broadway Books titles may be purchased for business or promotional use or for special sales. For information, please write to: Special Markets Department, Random House, Inc., 1745 Broadway, New York, NY 10019.

PRINTED IN THE UNITED STATES OF AMERICA

BROADWAY BOOKS and its logo, a letter B bisected on the diagonal, are trademarks of Broadway Books, a division of Random House, Inc.

Visit our website at www.broadwaybooks.com

First edition published 2003.

Designed by Bonni Leon-Berman
Illustrated by Ellen Sandbeck

Thank you to the Ramakrishna-Vivekananda Center of New York for permission to quote from *Vivekananda: The Yogas and Other Works,* published by the Ramakrishna-Vivekananda Center of New York; Copyright 1953 by Swami Nikhilananda, Trustee of the Estate of Swami Vivekananda.

Library of Congress Cataloging-in-Publication Data
Sandbeck, Ellen
Eat more dirt : diverting and instructive tips for growing and tending an organic garden / Ellen Sandbeck.
        p. cm.
ISBN 0-7679-0920-8
1. Organic gardening. I. Title.

SB453.5 .S26 2003
635'.0484—dc21   2003028221

10 9 8 7 6 5 4 3 2 1

To Grace Miller and Eleanor Nichol.
When I grow up I want to be just like you.
You are my shining lights.

CONTENTS

INTRODUCTION

There is a difference between working knowledge and a scientist's knowledge of a subject. Since the most active component of my memory is the forgetting part, working knowledge for me is just that—the knowledge that I use when working, plus the stuff that is so wonderfully odd or amusing that I can't forget it. This book contains some of each. It is of necessity an incomplete work. Gardening is a lifelong undertaking, a journey requiring the full engagement of mind, body, and spirit. Based on life expectancy statistics for the United States, I guess I am halfway there.

I really began working on this book in Oakland, California, in 1980, when my husband (then boyfriend) and I first began doing organic landscaping for a living. I very happily did library and field research and kept exhaustive notes. Two children, a move to Minnesota, and thirteen years later, a nonprofit group asked me to write a booklet on nontoxic gardening and housecleaning. I thought, "Oh, well, it isn't exactly what I was planning to write, but I'll do it." I had so much material that the booklet turned into a book: *Slug Bread & Beheaded Thistles: Amusing and Useful Techniques for Nontoxic Gardening and Housekeeping.*

My first shipment of *Slug Bread & Beheaded Thistles* arrived in 1995, and the first lesson I learned as a publisher was that being a publisher is a lot of work. I was overjoyed when Broadway Books acquired the rights to the book in 1999, and I was able to quit doing all the things I wasn't good at, like bookkeeping and publicity.

When the publisher wanted me to write another book, I dug out my old landscaping notes and rough manuscript. They were so completely humorless that they made me laugh. I promptly recycled them.

So there I was, at last, with a contract to write the book I had wanted to write for twenty years! Could life get any better than this? After a year of note-taking—winter research done while I walked on my elliptical trainer, and outdoor thoughts jotted down in work-pocket notepads—I reluctantly settled down indoors to begin the long task of transcribing my notes on September 10, 2001.

The next day four passenger planes were forced out of the sky, and everything else suddenly seemed completely irrelevant. I struggled for a long time to find reasons to continue my writing project. This book is the product of the conclusions I reached. I am including a couple of my notebook entries here, because I have utterly failed at doing anything with these writings beyond simply transcribing them:

SEPTEMBER 12, 2001

It is very hard to fathom why I should keep writing a book about gardening, in the light of yesterday's monstrosities. Why would anyone want to read such a book? But, during W.W. II there were "Victory Gardens," and I truly believe that all gardens are peace gardens. If we don't have something we love, believe in, and cherish in this living world, what will teach us love, empathy, and forgiveness? What will keep us from becoming destroyers?

SEPTEMBER 16, 2001

I drove into town this morning, after we had cleaned a chipmunk bed out of the glove compartment, in the company of a fly. I killed a mosquito on the windshield before I left, because I find mosquitoes to be a driving hazard, but after the horrendous events of the past week, I found myself feeling rather tender toward the fly. I know that flies can carry disease, but certainly if something happened, and only the fly and I were left alive, I would love that fly dearly until the end of one of our days. Life, in no matter what form, is precious.

We love that which we know intimately. No lover ever knew his beloved better than a gardener knows his garden. Learning to love a single small plot of earth is a good start toward learning to be protective of our beautiful little planet.

Chapter One

A Homegrown PARADISE

 our garden can either bring you bliss or drive you insane, and it is within your power to decide which it will do. This book is about a very specific type of garden: a paradise garden, which is designed to produce bliss. (It may also produce food, or flowers, but that is secondary to its main purpose.)

Over the decades that my husband and I have been landscaping organically, I have had the opportunity to work with a lot of homeowners. I have learned a lot about gardening and a lot about garden owners. I have repeatedly encountered homeowners whose gardens make them miserable. Unreasonable expectations play a big part in their misery. No matter how much we may wish otherwise, annuals do not live forever, sun-loving plants cannot thrive in shade, and blossoms eventually fade. Insects, wind storms, hail, and drought are all part of life on earth; gardening is a way to embrace life, not a way to control life. Life cannot be controlled, so learn all you can, try to keep your body in good working order, put in your best effort, then relax and enjoy the ride! (This sounds a lot like surfing, doesn't it?)

Over a decade ago we had an elderly neighbor who was made terribly unhappy by the deficiencies of her bleeding heart (*Dicentra spectabilis*), which grew on the shady side of her house. Each year she complained that it didn't bloom enough. We had a grand view of it from our living room window—it was the biggest, most beautiful, most floriferous *Dicentra* we had ever seen. The average garden-variety *Dicentra* blooms only for a month in the spring. Hers bloomed all spring, summer, and well into the fall. Perhaps our neighbor didn't realize that the plants with the biggest, splashiest flowers usually require large amounts of sun and heat, so every year she allowed herself to be disappointed that her shade plant wasn't blooming like a hothouse rose. As Francis Bacon said: "Knowledge is power." A corn farmer is not disappointed when his plants don't produce tomatoes.

So how do you go about designing your own little bit of paradise? First of all, you have to figure out what you want from your garden. Visiting as many gardens as possible is a good way to begin.

There really is nothing new under the sun, especially in gardening. While doing research for this book, I was amused to discover that every single garden idea I have ever had was at least several thousand years old. Amazingly, arbors, pergolas, flower beds, designs executed in colored gravel, garden statuary, clipped hedges, pavilions, terraces, decorative buildings, grottos, bridges, roof gardens, artificial plants, rock gardens, potted plants, fountains, garden ponds, and even heated swimming pools are just a few of the garden features that the ancients thought up first.

It is not as easy to design an enjoyable garden as it might seem; if it were easy, all gardens would make their proprietors happy. A good garden begins in the gardener's mind, and then is manifested on paper. I have to admit that when I am gardening for myself, I don't always draw up a plan. I have been gardening so long that I rather like improvisatory "jazz gardening," but I always have to make lists. Some of the lists I make are exactly the same as any garden design book would recommend: lists of favorite plants; lists of favorite colors; lists of structural features you want in your garden; and lists of what you want from your garden, such as summer shade, flowers, fruit, vegetables, space for children and pets to romp, a wildlife habitat, a peaceful place to meditate, and so forth.

Though I love strenuous gardening, most of the gardens I've designed and planted for clients have been low-maintenance ones. Our first home's garden evolved into an extremely well-balanced ecosystem that really didn't need me at all. We eventually had to move to a place with more land just to keep me from rattling around aimlessly. This experience made me realize that there was a list I had been neglecting: the favorite jobs list.

As Mark Twain wrote in *Letters from the Earth*: "By this time you will have noticed that the human being's heaven has been thought out and constructed upon an absolutely definite plan; and that this plan... shall contain, in labored detail, each and every imaginable thing that is repulsive to a man, and not a single thing that he likes!" If you replace *heaven* with *garden,* and *thing* is supplanted by *chore,* you will have a pretty accurate description of a large percentage of American yards.

Weekend after weekend, people plod patiently but joylessly behind lawn mowers, cutting the very grass they have fertilized into faster growth. Then they clip their shrubs into neat imitation gumdrops and rake the clippings out of the gravel bed below the shrubs. "Everything is interesting if you look at it deeply enough," said the late physicist Richard Feynman. But in my humble opinion, one has to look far too deeply at an all-lawn-and-hedge garden to make it interesting. I don't want to have to look at a garden through an electron microscope.

While putting my notes into some semblance of order for this book—"C" for community, "D" for dance, "Z" for Zen—I was amused to observe that a very high percentage of my notes were catalogued "P" for pleasure. It doesn't take a mind-boggling, hair-raising, death-defying experience to amuse me. My friends have often exclaimed, while laughing at me, "Easily amused!"

I am indeed easily amused, but there are some garden jobs that I don't find amusing at all. A garden should be, among other things, a refuge from the things that drive you crazy, a diversion from modern life's mostly indoor vexations.

One of our first clients, who I will refer to as Mrs. Fastidious, kept an extremely neat house and was trying desperately to control her yard as if it were an extension of her living room. She didn't like deciduous trees because they were "too messy." Even evergreens weren't quite up to her standards, because they eventually dropped needles into their gravel bed. Trying to keep a gravel bed completely free of organic debris is a task that would frustrate Sisyphus.

How to Keep a Garden from Being the Bane of Your Existence

Life is a process, not a product. Gardening is also a journey; if it is only enjoyable at its completion, what's the point? If your garden is beautiful only when it's been newly coiffed—its lawns newly manicured; its symmetrical hedges freshly clipped; its perfect show-quality tea roses with nary an aphid or splotch, and you hate lawn mowing and hedge trimming—your moments of happiness in the garden may be fleeting. The only perfect humans are dead—just talk to any living person's family, then read today's obituaries.

The people who get the most pleasure out of their gardens are those who really enjoy puttering around doing gardening chores. The beauty and utility of their gardens bring them great pleasure, but the sheer physical joy of work is just as important to them.

They garden to please themselves, not to impress, placate, or fit in with the neighbors.

I don't enjoy "tidying" jobs such as raking leaves out of gravel or off pavement; I can't stand listening to engine noise or inhaling exhaust, so I avoid using a power mower, leaf blower, or rototiller. I thrive on larger-scale physical labor: I love to lug things around by hand or wheelbarrow; dig and rake, saw and prune; mulch; and harvest fruits and vegetables. But most of all I find the compost pile endlessly fascinating.

Ellen's Garden Chore List

LIKES: heavy work; wheelbarrowing; lifting and carrying; digging; rock gardening; mulching; composting; leaf raking; sit-down weeding and transplanting; picking flowers, fruits, and vegetables
DISLIKES: mowing lawn; clipping hedges; using machinery; tidying gravel; raking pavement; weeding cracks in pavement

---

A list of the garden chores you enjoy and the chores you dislike may be the single most powerful tool you can employ when designing your garden. Give yourself the opportunity to do the kind of work you enjoy, and minimize the work you dislike. Let the garden's form follow your favorite functions.

Even if you tend to avoid heavy labor, there is much to be said for allowing room for strenuous jobs in your garden, jobs you can attack instead of inflicting damage on innocent bystanders when you are having a bad day. Brush hogging a tangled thicket is a great way to work out your frustrations, or if you want to use the technical term, "to get your ya-yas out."

Unless you enjoy the meditative value of picking leaves, twigs, evergreen needles, weeds, and litter out of gravel, I can't recommend decorative gravel beds. Our friend Sterling once pointed out to me that public gardens that feature shrubs and hedges in mulched beds are almost self-cleaning, because windblown litter tends to accumulate under the shrubs and decompose there.

I can't stand the sound of a rake on gravel, so in our yard ornamental gravel beds are out of favor. Nor do I like pulling weeds out of cracks in pavement, so if there is paving, I plant ground-covering herbs, or scatter the seeds of low-growing annuals in the cracks. Flowers and herbs like alyssum, violas, pansies, columbine, oregano, thyme, cosmos, and calendula all reproduce prolifically and, if your soil is healthy, can actually out-compete weeds. What a pleasure to find thyme or alyssum instead of quack grass growing up through the path! When I am in the mood for a sit-down job, I can scoot along on my posterior, dig up some of my flowering "weeds," and transplant them wherever I want them.

The Joy of Not Mowing the Lawn

It's not difficult to design a garden that gives me the opportunity to do the work I enjoy. If, like me, you don't enjoy lawn mowing, a minimal lawn or an "herbal lawn" can be quite appealing. Herbal lawns often include flowering ground covers such as creeping thyme, chamomile, *Mazus reptans*, violets, English lawn daisy (*Bellis perennis*), *Veronica repens*, and Irish and Scotch moss (*Sagina subulata*). Some grass species, for instance, the native buffalo grass (*Buchloë dactyloides*), are naturally low growers, and need mowing far less frequently than the more commonly used lawn grasses.

If you aren't planning to walk barefoot on your lawn, you can plant moss pink (*Phlox subulata*), which is a beautiful, tough, flowery little plant with extremely sharp needlelike leaves, and white Dutch clover (*Trifolium repens*), whose sweet-smelling flowers attract bees.

If you aren't planning to walk on your lawn at all, your possibilities expand enormously. There are many tough ground covers that easily out-compete weeds. Flowering scented herbs such as thyme, yarrow, mints, and oregano are pretty, useful, and good spreaders, which don't mind being stepped on occasionally. Planting these tough herbs can be a wonderful way to avoid the hazards of mowing a steep sunny slope. Some succulent little ground-covering sedums spread extremely quickly, sending out roots from their sprawling stems as well as from every fleshy little leaf that breaks off the mother plant. Sedums cannot tolerate any traffic at all, but require no upkeep. Lily of the valley makes a wonderful ground cover for shady areas. Talk to other gardeners and visit nurseries in your area to determine which hardy ground covers will be the best for you.

There are also a lot of low-growing "weeds" that are tough as nails. You may discover some of them growing in high-traffic areas where the grass has been worn off. Before we had a chance to pave one of our well-trodden paths, a beautiful green crop of knotgrass (*Polygonum aviculare*) filled in the bare, packed-down trail. (Knotgrass is not grass. It is related to rhubarb.) I pulled it out until I realized that its fine-textured leaves made it a good lawn substitute for a very difficult area.

If you are one of the many people who enjoys lawn mowing, you can make the process more environmentally sound by using a nonmotorized lawn mower and planting well-adapted grasses that don't require much fertilizer or watering. If no one in your family is allergic to bee stings, a mixed clover and grass lawn is far tougher than an all-grass lawn; the clover stays green through the driest weather, and the nitrogen-rich clover clippings will fertilize the grass every time you mow.

If you really enjoy mowing grass and clipping hedges, and live in a rainy climate, by all means plant lots of lawn and lots of hedges. Enjoy yourself while you cut. You will generate a lot of fodder for the compost heap. But if you don't enjoy mowing and trimming, plant what you enjoy playing with.

The (Dis)Harmony of the Shrubs

Keep in mind that perfect control is not possible in a garden: nature will intrude. Hail, wind, drought, unseasonable freezes, and animals will eventually cause damage in almost every garden. Perfect symmetry is very difficult to maintain: plants die, branches break, and a perfectly even box hedge develops gaps. Unless you have planted replacement box plants somewhere on your vast estate, the hedge's symmetry is gone for good. This can be very frustrating.

If you really crave symmetry but don't have the manpower to maintain topiaries and replacement hedges, try using nonliving elements like statuary, trellises, paths, arbors, ponds, or large flowerpots for your symmetry. Your frustration level will be far lower than if you attempt that ancient Roman urban gardening style.

The prototypical formal "urban" garden was invented in ancient Rome. It featured paved terraces, geometrical and highly formal beds edged with clipped evergreen hedges, topiaries, and statuary. The Roman "manicured" look screamed, "Look! I have slaves!" because it was so incredibly labor intensive. The manicured look is still very energy intensive, though these days a lot of the work is accomplished with machines and chemicals.

The costs of hands-off gardening are still at least as high as they were in Pliny's day, when he complained: "He whose fields are cultivated in his absence by slave labor, agitates his fields and cultivates his own future desperation." The desperation Pliny was referring to included loss of topsoil, loss of fertility, and erosion induced by agriculture and logging. Modern agriculture still suffers from the old complaints, but has added chemically polluted soil, air, and water to the ancient list.

Intergardener Relations

When a garden is owned and worked in by more than one person, work lists need to be compared and coordinated so everyone gets a chance to do what they like in the garden. Unfortunately, as my husband and I learned on several occasions while trying to design gardens for clients, married couples don't always want the same things. May I humbly suggest that if blue flowers mortally depress you, and yellow cheers and sustains you, so that you feel you really *must* have a yellow garden, even though your spouse is made queasy by yellow and prefers blue, you may have some work to do outside of the garden.

Even though gardening can be too hot, too cold, dirty, dusty, sweaty, mosquito-ridden, heartbreaking, discouraging, and infuriating, it is also incredibly romantic. The only way to take the romance out of gardening is to take the fun out of it: plant a garden that requires a huge amount of the kind of work you don't enjoy, and you will have turned a love affair into a job.

My husband and I have spent almost our entire courtship and subsequent marriage gardening together. We landscape together for a living and were married in a botanical garden. Our children had gardening jobs as soon as they could toddle: pruning dead bits off clients' shrubs with a dull pruner. Love, gardening, and romance are for me inextricably linked.

Romance is not straight-edged, concrete-walled, or contained in bender board. It is a bit messy, full of unexpected life, not completely domesticated, and imperfect. The Mississippi River is romantic because it is big and resists all attempts to tame it; a concrete-bedded, straightened river is not romantic, nor is it healthy. Romance requires the unknown, mystery, the unknowable.

The Amazing, Astounding, Expanding, Stress-Reducing Garden

Imparting mystery to a garden doesn't necessarily require a lot of space. Our friend Alice, a retired medical researcher, has a beautiful woodland garden, complete with a boardwalk, a pond, and a little bridge. Alice knows exactly what she needs in a garden: "I walk around my garden every morning; it sometimes takes me ten minutes. [Alice has a very small yard.] It makes me feel relaxed and happy the rest of the day, no matter how tense I started out.

It's best to have plants tucked into all kinds of nooks and crannies, then I can poke around and find my wild ginger, and feel a thrill if it's blooming."

It is the richness and diversity of her plantings that allow Alice to lose herself in her garden; if it were less beautiful, circumambulating her garden would take about twenty seconds. Alice tries out new shade-loving perennials every year. "Throw in a lot of things, and the garden will look fine even if some plants get eaten," says Alice.

Alice's garden is successful because she has learned to accept the fact that her yard has no sun at all. She has stopped trying to plant anything that needs sun, partial sun, or even partial shade. "My next-door neighbor complains that it's so shady that nothing blooms and nothing grows. She is standing in the sun in her yard while she's saying this. My yard has no sun at all."

A Homegrown Paradise

I have been extremely lucky: my idea of Paradise is to work with my loved ones in a wildly exuberant garden, which produces an abundance of healthy plants and small creatures to be admired and cooed over, and this is exactly what I have. The garden you love may not resemble other people's idea of a garden at all, but if it brings you happiness, it is a completely successful garden. Some Zen gardens contain no plants at all, just rocks and raked sand. The owner of an extensive and expensive collection of rare conifers is not necessarily happier than the gardener whose paths are edged with rows of teakettles planted with marigolds. Plant what you love in your garden. You reap what you sow.

This winter, one of our neighbors is cultivating ravens. He has a fine crop of them in his trees now, which he attracted to his woods with some offal from a recently butchered steer. He and his family can watch the birds from their kitchen window. There is a great deal of joy to be had in a bumper crop of ravens.

 *When I was an art student in college, I took a class that featured a different guest artist teaching every week. One of the guests had the class do an exercise that made an enormous impression on me: we all walked to the beach together; our guest artist was carrying a brown paper bag and refused to tell us what was in it until we got to the beach. We formed a circle, then she opened the bag and showed us the carnations inside. Half of them were red, half were white. She told us that the red carnations symbolized Beauty and the white ones symbolized Truth, and that we had to choose. If we chose Beauty, we should take a red carnation, if we chose Truth, we should take a white carnation. "Now choose!" she said. Everyone grabbed. Of the twenty or so people in the circle, including the teacher, only two chose red carnations. The other red carnation and I were ridiculed and derided by the other students: "How could you possibly choose anything but Truth? How can you be that immature? What is wrong with you?"*

We outcasts huddled together for support and discussed it later: I had chosen the red carnation because I really like red carnations and didn't want a white one. She had done the same. We hadn't chosen Beauty; we had chosen beauty.

What is the Truth? I don't know, but I think it is possible that some of the other people on the beach went home with a carnation in a color they didn't like.

Uncommon Garden Variety

The gardener's ingenuity is what makes a garden beautiful and interesting and fun. Necessity is the mother of invention and, at the very least, the best friend of an interesting garden.

Any hollow object, natural or man-made, can be, and probably already has been, used as a planter. Garden paths have been paved with everything from broken seashells to broken glass set into concrete. Garden sculptures can range from classical statuary to giant welded steel insects. There really is nothing common about "garden variety."

Last summer I passed a tiny house with a small yard filled with a sea of tall cosmos, with a few bachelor's buttons gleaming below, and several birdhouses peeking up like periscopes. It was the most cheerful garden I have ever seen, and very far from being formal.

Even the most "tailored, manicured" garden can benefit from having some area that is "wild." Many gardens already have areas like this, on the "lost" side of the house, near the faucet, for example. Observing these untended areas can help a gardener learn more about her garden's particular ecosystem. Hedgerows, which break up the blank perfection of fields, are also what break up the wind, preventing dust storm catastrophes, and the weeds that grow in and near hedgerows harbor beneficial predatory insects as well as other insectivorous critters.

There are injunctions in the Bible about not harvesting the corners of the field; and Zen Buddhism mandates a flaw in each tea ceremony teacup (lest the potter insinuate he's perfect).

Gardener's Manners

There are two main principles by which I garden: *Do no harm* and *Garden to please yourself.*

The idea of doing no harm is relative. We can only do our best. Every breath we take kills airborne microorganisms; we crush small creatures beneath our feet with every step; our every bite of food once lived. When we decide to keep on living, we make the decision to take the lives of other organisms. The huge amount of nutrient-laden runoff that flows from the Mississippi River into the Gulf of Mexico, though disastrous for most marine life, is a great boon for algae.

As Swami Vivekananda, the great spokesman for Hinduism, wrote over a century ago: "All work is by nature composed of good and evil. We cannot do any work which will not do some good somewhere; there cannot be any work which will not cause some harm somewhere. Every work must necessarily be a mixture of good and evil. Yet we are commanded to work incessantly. Good and evil will both have their results, will bear their fruit."

The Organic Gardener's Pledge

1. *Protect and preserve the land and the waters*
2. *Leave no ground bare: cover it with mulch and / or ground-covering plants*
3. *Build up your soil*
4. *Do not disturb the soil unnecessarily; try to preserve its layers intact and right side up*
5. *Compost*
6. *Avoid the use of synthetic chemicals*
7. *Utilize plant materials that are appropriate to your climate*
8. *Avoid planting aggressive, invasive nonnative plants*
9. *Preserve valuable plant specimens*
10. *Please yourself—do not garden with your neighbor's reaction in mind*

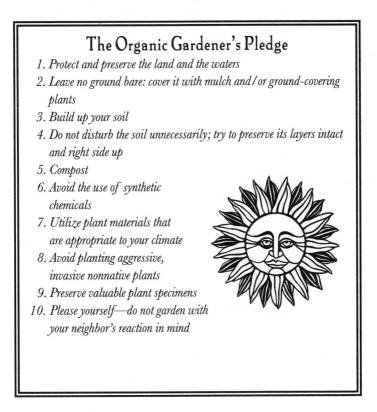

Chapter Two

Don't Pave
PARADISE

aradise is a state of mind, not a physical address. The garden that colors your fantasies may not be possible to create in your climate. If you cannot survive without fishing, water-skiing, and birches, *don't move to Arizona!* The paper birches you plant to remind you of home will not thrive, and your efforts to make the desert produce birches will gravely damage the fragile desert environment. If enough people plant water-hungry plants in an arid area, and then keep the plants alive by watering them heavily, humidity levels will increase while groundwater stores decrease. This is paradise for some, perhaps, but at a terrible price. It is wonderful that our country is so full of beautiful, majestic scenery, but we can't all live on top of it. Not everyone can live on the beach, or in the very best spot for viewing the mountains, or the natural integrity of these places will be ruined. The hills I hiked as a girl are now private property and off limits to hikers.

An organic landscape is not merely one that is grown without synthetic chemicals; "organic" also refers to something that is an integral part of the whole. A truly organic landscape should be well enough adapted to its climate that the plants can survive largely on their own. The organic gardener and her garden are part of, not apart from, the environment. Unfortunately, we have a very long way to go before our society's agricultural and gardening efforts become an organic part of our environment. In the summer of 1956, for the first time ever, water from the Colorado River did not reach the Gulf of California: U.S. agricultural water use had drained the river before it reached the Gulf. Currently, across the United States, an estimated 25 to 50 percent of residential water use goes to maintaining landscapes.

There are natural laws that determine the way our universe runs; some people would argue that these laws were set up by God, others argue that these laws *are* God, and still others state that these laws are laws and that is all. The gardener establishes the natural law of the garden: her practices determine the direction in which the garden will run. These practices can make the difference between a well-balanced garden that increases in health and productivity, and an unbalanced garden with declining health. As the fox said to the Little Prince in the classic children's story by Antoine de Saint-Exupéry: "It is the time you have wasted for your rose that makes your rose so important," and "You become responsible forever, for what you have tamed. You are responsible for your rose...."

One evening as I was annoying my husband by reading National Geographic *over his shoulder, the old adage "You are what you eat" leapt to my mind. The magazine was open to a beautiful photo of a grizzly waiting at the top of a small waterfall for a huge leaping trout to land in its open mouth. The trout was so precisely the same color as the water that it looked like a fish-shaped piece of waterfall.*

Healthy fish require healthy water; deformed fish and frogs are the product of deformed water. Researchers studying Chinook salmon from the Columbia River recently discovered that 84 percent of the fish that appeared to be female were actually genetically male. Endocrine-disrupting pollutants in the river are emasculating the male salmon. Some ponds in agricultural areas are producing six-legged, one-eyed frogs, along with other odd variations on the standard frog form, and no one seems to know exactly why.

When I was in junior high school, the dangers of the insecticide DDT were just being discovered. Birds were cracking their own eggs by sitting on them, and the bald eagle was in danger of becoming extinct. Now that DDT has largely been banned, the bald eagle is making a comeback (we have often spied bald eagles flying overhead as we drive home, and occasionally we've seen them feasting on roadkill by the side of the road).

Gardening impacts the world at large, not just the gardener and those who garden with her. Fertilizers and pesticides rarely stay put. We once saw the sun-bleached corpse of a large orange tree that had died when weeds in a patio twenty feet away were sprayed with herbicide. The weeds' progeny were still thriving in the patio. Unfortunately, synthetic chemicals prove the point that it's a small world: many synthetic chemicals are extremely volatile, and have been detected in even the most remote regions of the earth.

Even water, that most innocuous of substances, can cause problems.

Though the Southwest is the most arid region of the United States, its population is growing much faster than that of the rest of the country. The most flamboyant example of this is Las Vegas, the fastest-growing city in the United States. Approximately five thousand people move to Las Vegas each month; by February of 2001, its population had swelled to 1.4 million.

Las Vegas is located in the middle of the Mojave Desert. Its annual rainfall is about four inches, making it the driest large city in the United States. By 1962, the springs near Las Vegas had all dried up. Now, 88 percent of Las Vegas's water comes from the Colorado River. According to the Southern Nevada Water Authority, the average Las Vegas resident uses 360 gallons of water per day—more than three times the national average of 101 gallons per day. Residents of Tucson, Arizona, have a comparatively moderate per capita water use of about 160 gallons per day.

When most of us think of Las Vegas, we think of casinos, many of which have huge fountains and pools. But the casinos use up far less of Las Vegas's water supply than one might think. I was amazed to learn that the resorts use only 8 percent of Las Vegas's water; private residences use far more. In the summer, 90 percent of the water utilized by private citizens in Las Vegas is used outside, mainly to water lawns; in the winter the percentage drops to 70 percent.

The Gulf of California, the end of the line for the Colorado River, has been suffering from the effects of water diversion for the past seventy years. The tidal flats of the Colorado River delta depend upon the influx of nutrient-rich fresh water from the river itself. These wetlands have shrunk from their original 1.9 million acres to 150,000 acres, and their marine life has been virtually wiped out from lack of nutrients.

The population of shellfish in the estuary is now only about 5 percent of what it was before the water diversions began. Many different organisms, ranging from migratory waterfowl to shrimp fishermen, depend upon the shellfish for their livelihood and are suffering.

Researchers have noted that in years following water releases from upstream reservoirs, shrimp catches have been higher in the Northern Gulf of California. A 1999 Environmental Defense Fund study concluded that the Colorado River delta needs 100,000 acre feet, or 32.6 billion gallons, of water per year in order to maintain the remnant of its ecosystem. (An acre foot of water equals 326,000 gallons.) Las Vegas's lawns alone use about 147 billion gallons of Colorado River water per year.

Whether you are animal, vegetable, or mineral, if you can't stand the heat, don't move to the desert.

On the other side of Mexico, the Gulf of Mexico is also suffering, but from too many nutrients rather than too few. Every summer since it first appeared in the 1950s, a terrifying phenomenon called the "Dead Zone" has occurred in the Gulf off the coast of Louisiana: an almost total lack of oxygen in the water kills whatever marine life cannot flee. The Dead Zone has increased greatly in size every year since it was first mapped in 1985, and since the late 1990s has covered over 7,000 square miles each summer.

There are nine Dead Zones worldwide, with the largest occurring in the Gulf of Mexico. They are the result of an overabundance of dissolved mineral nutrients, especially nitrogen, which feeds enormous algal blooms. These masses of algae eventually die, and the vast amount of organic material is broken down by bacteria, which use up almost all the available oxygen during the process of decomposition.

The Mississippi River basin drains 41 percent of the continental United States, and is home to 70 million people. The Dead Zone is caused by human activities: chemical fertilizers and other contaminents that are washed into the Mississippi and its tributaries from farmlands and domestic landscapes. Buildings and pavement are not absorbent; so as farmland, woods, and wetlands are "developed," the land's capacity to absorb water and nutrients diminishes.

The coastal wetlands of Louisiana contain approximately 40 percent of all salt marshes in the lower forty-eight states, and Louisiana provides 25 to 30 percent of the nation's seafood. In the summer, Louisiana's calm coastal waters serve as a nursery for juvenile shrimp, fish, and other sea life, but this nursery area is sometimes in the rotten heart of the Dead Zone.

We don't have to understand everything scientifically in order to protect our land. We just need to care deeply about it, as we do about our children. We need to be vigilant and observant, and ever ready to change our ways if we sense danger.

More than twenty-four centuries ago, people knew that allowing excess fertilizer to run off the land was not a good idea: Theophrastus, a Greek natural scientist and philosopher, wrote that it is not advisable to add more nutrients than the land can hold: "It is better to manure a little and often than in excess."

Wham, Bam, Thank You, Ma'am

Like the villains in old-fashioned melodramas, chemical fertilizers tend to work quickly, then run off. Compost and other organic fertilizers are like old-fashioned heroes: slow, steady, and stable.

The Environmental Protection Agency (EPA) estimates that excess nutrient flow into the Mississippi must drop by 40 percent to eliminate the annual Dead Zone. We are all partially responsible for the problem. One gardener spreading one too many bags of fertilizer on a lawn is a drop in the nutrient bucket; several million gardeners overfertilizing their lawns add up. If you use commercial fertilizers, whether organic or chemical, please read and follow the label directions. More is not better. Chemical fertilizers are like heroin for plants: there's a quick rush, then a sudden drop into weakness and dependency. Eventually the plants require more and more fertilizer to achieve the same results. Organic fertilizer, on the other hand, is a food, not a drug.

Inch by Inch

I can't do much as an individual about starving children in Asia and Africa, the depletion of the ozone layer, or just about any other global problem I can imagine. And the environmentally perfect house constructed of all recycled materials, powered solely by solar panels and a wind generator, and the solar-electric car are a bit out of my financial reach at the moment. But changing the landscape is *easy*! Your lawn will change if you simply stop watering and fertilizing it. A gravel lawn spray-painted with non-toxic green dye or an Astroturf lawn is better for the environment than a well-watered, fertilized, pesticide-treated lawn. But if you decide that an inert garden does not appeal to you, the real adventure can begin.

Chapter Three

Growing
HEALTHY
SOIL

 *uckily, organic gardening is far easier than* rocket science, or, I assure you, I would not be doing it. "Organic," in this context, means gardening using only fertilizers, soil conditioners, pesticides, and herbicides that are composed of naturally occurring plant, animal, or mineral materials. Though the chemical definition of "organic" is anything containing carbon, gardeners do not consider petroleum products or other artificially produced carbon compounds "organic" for the purposes of gardening.

I concentrate far more on increasing the health and fertility of the soil than I do on pampering the plants living in it. (I don't like being pampered myself; my husband quickly figured out that the best way to get me up on a weekend morning is to offer to bring me breakfast in bed.) I like plants that are hardy and well adapted and can mostly fend for themselves. If you do enjoy pampering plants, situating them in healthy soil is the nicest thing you can do for them.

Healthy Soil Means Healthy People

If we were paying attention, we would be more protective of our topsoil. It takes a thousand years for one centimeter of soil to form on bare lava in Hawaii, and even longer for soil to form in cold climates. But instead of treating our topsoil like gold, we have been treating it like dirt.

When left in their natural state, soils generally increase in depth and fertility, barring natural disasters like fire, landslides, and volcanic eruptions. The enormous fertility of virgin soils can fool farmers into believing that they can take from the soil indefinitely without giving anything back.

The oldest existing Greek and Roman books on agriculture reveal that the earliest Greek and Roman farmers did not consider fertilizing their fields important. Here is a perfect illustration of this archaic attitude: one of Hercules' Twelve Labors was to clean King Augeias' stables, which had not been mucked out for many years. Hercules flushed the manure out of the stables by diverting two rivers through them. Reading this myth makes me wince. What a depressing waste of good manure!

There is, as everybody knows, no such thing as a free lunch: if organic material is removed from the soil in the form of crops and crop residues, and never replaced, the soil will gradually lose fertility. Farmers in ancient Greece and Rome

eventually experienced what happens when the soil is farmed but not fed.

The Greek philosopher Plato (427–347 B.C.) understood that dense vegetation prevented erosion and that stable soils absorb water quickly and release it slowly, reducing flooding and allowing streams and rivers to run year-round. Unfortunately, by the time the Greeks understood these things, it was too late: Greece had already been deforested and farmed hard, much of her topsoil had washed off the hills, some of her springs had dried up, and many streams and rivers ran only during the rainy season.

NOW FOR THE MILLION-DOLLAR question: If the importance of soil conservation was understood in the Old World at least by the first century B.C., how did we end up with the Dust Bowl in the 1930s? What happened to all that knowledge?

People tend to forget information and skills that they are not using. In this age of calculators and personal computers, how many people still know how to use slide rules? When was the last time anyone actually used a trigonometry table?

When European immigrants first plowed the land in the New World, the soil had enormous stores of organic material; the yields of the newly plowed soil were huge. The farmers didn't realize that they were decreasing the fertility of the land every time they plowed. The soil seemed inexhaustible, and it didn't occur to them that they needed to give some fertility back.

The new immigrants also didn't realize that they were benefitting from the good husbandry of the Native Americans they had displaced. Tilling the soil was an uncommon practice among Native Americans, who regarded the earth as their mother and were disturbed by the thought of cutting into her flesh.

Lawrence Svobida, a young Kansas farmer, kept a diary during the devastation of the Dust Bowl, and published it as *An Empire of Dust* in 1940. Through setback after setback—hailstorms, dust storms, insects, and drought—Svobida kept working as long and as hard as he possibly could. Day after day, often during blinding,

choking dust storms, he kept discing, plowing, harrowing, planting, and replanting, struggling to save his land. Then, at the very last, when nothing was left, when all his topsoil had blown away and someone else's dust was choking his fields, he finally realized that everything he had been doing, everything he had been taught to do, was wrong.

There were a couple of signs that he didn't understand, and neither did any of the other farmers. One was that even when the wheat crops failed, the weeds still grew; the weeds were far better adapted to harsh conditions than were the crops. Because Svobida "knew" that weeds were bad, he put himself on a "sunup until dark" schedule on his tractor, cultivating to kill weeds.

The hapless farmer didn't realize that many weeds specialize in protecting bare soil. If the weeds had been allowed to live, they might have helped save some of the thousands of square miles of topsoil that blew off the Great Plains during the years of the Dust Bowl.

An elderly doctor in southwestern Nebraska wrote the following in his diary in the 1930s: "Wind forty miles an hour and hot as Hell. Two Kansas farms go by every minute."

> *Last week farmers in ten Midwestern States had sand in their beards, in their hair, in their ears, in their eyes, in their mouths, in their pockets, in their pants, in their boots, in their milk, coffee, soup and stew. Dust poured through the cracks in farmhouse walls, under the doors, down the chimneys. In northwest Oklahoma a hundred families fled their homes. Every school in Baca County, Colo., was closed. In Texas the windswept hayfields were alive with blinded sparrows.*
> —Time, April 22, 1935

Natural processes do not change. As long as there is wind and water, bare soil will be vulnerable to erosion. We may pat ourselves on the back, believing that we are too modern to suffer from the effects of another Dust Bowl, but the Dust Bowl farmers also believed they were modern.

Dust does not respect international borders. Dust particles are so small that they can reach altitudes of ten thousand feet. In 2001, satellites belonging to the National Aeronautics and Space Administration (NASA) and the National Oceanic and Atmospheric Administration (NOAA) tracked Saharan dust clouds as they crossed the Atlantic Ocean and settled into the Gulf of Mexico near Florida. Researchers linked the dust clouds with incidences of "red tides" and determined that iron in the African dust fertilizes the massive blooms of toxic algae that cause red tides. Red tides are deadly to marine life and can trigger skin and respiratory problems in human swimmers, as well as paralysis and memory problems in people who eat shellfish from red tide–contaminated water.

A record-breaking Chinese dust cloud formed in April of 2001, blacking out the sun in the northern Chinese province of Jilin. NASA tracked this dust cloud as it traveled across the Pacific Ocean, then across North America, darkening skies and depositing dust from Alaska to Florida, and finally subsided in the middle of the Atlantic Ocean. Chinese dust

clouds are a relatively new phenomenon; recent deforestation and the expansion of agriculture are exposing fragile areas to erosion.

Researchers using data from NASA satellites have recently discovered that large amounts of airborne dust, smoke particles, or urban air pollution can reduce rainfall and cause or exacerbate drought. We live on a small planet. Our air pollution can dirty skies and decrease rainfall in Europe. Africa's cattle herds kick up dust that not only reduces the rainfall in Africa but perhaps also in Florida. Dust-borne chemicals used on farms in China are deposited on the west coast of the United States.

Scientists studying chaos theory inform us that a butterfly flapping its wings in Beijing can affect the weather a month later in New York. How much more impact do we gardeners have on the world?

I recently excavated the sedimentary layers of my desk and found an article entitled "Better Living Through Chaos" (*The Economist*, September 18, 1999). I chuckled as I picked my way over piles of books in the study, secure in the knowledge that I am practicing the chaos that I preach.

Tiny Friends in Low Places

A multitude of creatures inhabits healthy soil. The combined weight of the mammals, reptiles, amphibians, worms, insects, bacteria, and fungi that live in the soil can be from five thousand to twenty thousand pounds per acre.

Soil fungi and bacteria break down dead plants and animals, producing humus in the process and freeing up nutrients for the use of plants. Healthy soil contains at least 10 percent humus and is home to billions of soil bacteria.

Many plants have a symbiotic relationship with fungi that live in and around their roots. The fungi deliver nutrients, especially nitrogen, to the roots and receive sugars from the roots in return. Many plants would starve to death without their fungi.

Though the common earthworm, like the majority of Americans, is not native to this country, earthworms are, nonetheless, active and useful inhabitants of our continent. Worm castings, which come out the back end of worms, contain five times the nitrogen, seven times the available phosphorus, eleven times more potash, and 40 percent more humus (decomposed organic material) than is usually found in the top six inches of the soil. Under favorable conditions, worms produce up to ten tons of castings per acre per year. There can be up to six million worm channels in an acre of cultivated soil, and up to half of the soil's air capacity down to a depth of four inches can be worm channels and tunnels.

Soil ecologist John N. Klironomos and coworker Miranda M. Hart, while trying to discover whether tiny soil-dwelling insects called springtails can damage trees by eating their symbiotic fungi, made an amusing discovery. When they tried feeding the eastern white pine's root fungi to the springtails, almost all of the insects died: the fungus paralyzed the springtails, then grew filaments into them to suck out all the delicious springtail nutrients. It appears that the fungi are active hunters of nitrogenous prey, not mere scavengers.

I have recently begun to think of myself as an ecosystem, a very small one as ecosystems go, but an ecosystem nonetheless. I began thinking this way after reading that an adult human body is made up of approximately ten trillion cells. I was particularly entranced to learn that my cells are outnumbered ten to one by the microorganisms that live in and on my body.

I have never considered myself to be much of a materialist, but I find that I am particularly proud of my assemblage of microbes. Though I did not possess a single microbe before I was born, I now boast a collection of approximately one hundred trillion microorganisms, which live on my skin and in my digestive, respiratory, and reproductive systems. My gut alone houses two or three hundred different species of bacteria as well as assorted viruses and parasites. (If you are squeamish about the thought of parasites, you may be less so by the time you get to the end of this chapter.) Bacteria in my large intestine produce B vitamins as well as vitamin K, which I absorb and utilize.

If you are lucky, you also possess a comprehensive collection of microorganisms. If you do not, your health may not be what it should be. Studies have shown that the incidence of asthma and allergies is increasing in industrialized nations worldwide. At the beginning of the twentieth century only one percent of the European population had allergies. By the end of the century between 15 and 20 percent of the European population had allergies; and in the United States there was a 75 percent increase in asthma cases between 1980 and 1994.

In an allergic reaction, the body is attempting to kill or expel a foreign protein; unfortunately, the protein the body is attacking is actually harmless, while the body's reaction to it is not. An allergic reaction could be compared to damage by "friendly fire": a naive and nervous soldier (the immune system), who has never actually encountered the enemy, senses a presence, becomes alarmed, and mistakes a harmless intruder for the enemy. The soldier (the immune system) then begins wildly firing his weapon (an immune reaction), wounding his own platoon (the body). The immune system, like a soldier, needs seasoning.

Many researchers now believe that the immune system is strengthened and matured through interaction with worms, bacteria, viruses, and other pathogens. The "hygiene hypothesis," first introduced in 1989, postulates that overly clean households can predispose children to develop allergies.

Numerous studies have shown that children from large families, farm children, children who started going to day care at a young age, and children with dogs, cats, or pigs in their homes are all less likely to have allergies than are children in more fastidious homes. What these lucky children all have in common is early exposure to microbes: farm children are more likely to play outside and encounter dirt, children in large families and children attending day care get colds from each other, and children with pets are exposed to animal dander and the microbes that live in the dander. Some researchers believe that this early exposure to dirt, dust, dander, and disease helps youngsters' immune systems mature and learn the difference between friend and foe. Without this early toughening up, a child may never develop a tolerance for this beautiful, disorderly world, and be doomed to living in a carpet-free, dust-free, pet-free house forever.

Researchers reported in the May 13, 2000, issue of the Lancet *that they had found a direct correlation between exposure to house dust and the development of allergies and asthma in allergy-prone infants. But before you panic and begin zealously cleaning your house, you should know that infants in the most dust-free homes had the highest incidence of allergies and asthma.*

Researchers chose sixty-one asthma-prone infants ages nine to twenty-four months for their study, then collected dust from the infants' homes using a vacuum with a screen over the nozzle.

The babies were tested for sensitization to airborne allergens: pollen, dust mites, cats, dogs, mice, cockroaches; and to foods: milk, eggs, or soya. When the researchers analyzed their data, they found that the babies who lived in dusty homes were far less likely to suffer from allergies and asthma than were the babies who lived in dust-free homes.

After decades of attempting to eradicate all tiny life-forms in our homes, gardens, and bodies, we must finally admit that we don't know which organisms are expendable and which are not. We are learning the hard way that we need a good, lively, diverse batch of microorganisms both inside and out in order to be healthy. I am not trying to suggest that we don't need cleanliness, because we do: we need to make sure our kitchens and bathrooms are clean, that we fully cook our meat, and wash our hands (with plain soap, not the antibacterial kind!) before cooking or eating. As Franklin Roosevelt said: "The only thing we have to fear is fear itself."

So let them eat dirt! And yogurt! And dust! And kiss the dog! And tease the cat! Let them make mud pies with real strawberries in them!

People often laugh when I use the term "good clean dirt." Many people think "good clean dirt" is an oxymoron, but I don't agree: good clean dirt is lively, healthy dirt, with a thriving population of microorganisms and a large supply of organic material to feed its tiny troops. It warms a mother's heart to watch her babies play in this kind of dirt.

A caveat about babies and dirt: Never let them crawl around where there are droppings from wild or domestic animals. Animal droppings can transmit extremely dangerous parasites to humans.

---

*"Nobody likes me, everybody hates me,
I'm gonna eat some worms!"*
ANONYMOUS, CHILDREN'S SONG

Actually, they're drinking them.

Joel Weinstock, director of the Digestive Disease Center at the University of Iowa Hospitals and Clinics, headed a study, published in 1999, in which volunteers drank Gatorade laced with the microscopic eggs of an intestinal worm. The worm, called porcine whipworm, normally infects pigs but not people. The worms can survive in the human intestine but can't reproduce.

Some of these volunteers drank worm eggs every three weeks for more than two years. Why in the world would anyone volunteer to ingest worm eggs? The answer is that the volunteers were desperate, all suffering from inflammatory bowel disease (IBD), a term that encompasses ulcerative colitis and Crohn's disease.

After ingesting the eggs, all the patients improved substantially. Most went into complete remission and were able to throw away their drugs, many of which had serious side effects. The symptoms returned when the patients stopped drinking the mixture.

Inflammatory bowel disease usually attacks victims in their late teens or twenties, and lasts a lifetime. Sufferers are afflicted with abdominal pain, diarrhea, and gastrointestinal bleeding. Part of the intestine may need to be surgically removed because of blockage caused by scarring; many patients require multiple surgeries. The cause of IBD is unknown and there is no known cure. The incidence of IBD has gone up substantially in the United States and Europe in the past sixty years, yet it is rare in poor countries where much of the population is infected with parasitic worms. An animal study led by David Elliott, M.D., at the University of Iowa, showed that mice which were specially bred to develop inflammatory bowel disease failed to develop the affliction when they were infected with intestinal worms.

I am extremely attached to my intestine, and would like to stay that way. Bring on the worms!

Gardener's Gold

The real difference between dirt and topsoil is humus, the "black gold" of the garden. Humus is a brown, slimy substance made up of the decomposed bodies of defunct plants, animals, and bacteria. It glues soil particles together into larger particles, allowing air channels to form between particles. Air and water can then enter the soil freely through these channels.

Humus is a very slow-acting, steady fertilizer. Soil bacteria, billions to the acre, break humus down into simpler chemicals that plants can utilize. When these billions of soil bacteria die, they become part of the humus.

A really rich soil has many of the same characteristics as a good chocolate cake: dark in color, a springy yet crumbly texture, and a divine fragrance. If you really want to make a gardener happy, tell her: "Your soil is just like devil's food cake." (I'm not sure the converse would be true for most bakers, however.)

Humus is what gives topsoil its "fluff." As its humus content decreases, soil becomes progressively denser and heavier, until it eventually reverts to weathered rock. Tilling the soil temporarily increases its fluffiness and makes it resemble rich topsoil, but the very act of cultivating further diminishes the soil. Any form of digging increases the amount of oxygen in the soil. This extra oxygen combines with and breaks down organic material in the soil, releasing its stored plant nutrients. Though plants temporarily benefit from the released nutrients, the structure of the soil suffers.

Many years of removing organic material in the form of weeds, leaves, and other garden residue can also impoverish garden soil. I have seen tomatoes struggling to grow in pale soil with only slightly more "fluff" than concrete, while only a few blocks away woodland plants were luxuriating in deep, dark, fertile topsoil.

If its organic material is not regularly replaced, soil will eventually go downhill. (If you garden on a hill, your soil will quite literally go downhill.)

Adding humus to clay soil is the only reasonable way to improve its drainage; mixing sand in with clay soil produces an aggregate that is extraordinarily like concrete. Adding humus to sandy soil increases the soil's water-holding capabilities and greatly improves its fertility. (It is hardly possible to decrease the fertility of sandy soil.) The structure of healthy soil also allows moisture to move up from deeper levels when the surface begins to dry out. This "wicking action" helps plants survive drought.

Loose material on the surface of the soil (also known as mulch) is disconnected from the soil's wicking action. Though water seeps down through mulch, it does not come back up easily, so mulch helps slow the evaporation of soil moisture. Though many different materials can be used as mulch, only organic materials will help build up the soil. One of the main reasons for plowing, tilling, or cultivating the soil is to create a loose mulch of dust to mimic the effect of an organic mulch. But since turning the soil actually diminishes its fertility, adding an organic mulch, which adds humus to the soil, is far preferable.

According to soil scientists, humus may be the most chaotic, disorderly, irregular material on earth (and in earth). "It is very possible that no two humus molecules are or ever have been alike," said soil scientist Dr. James Rice. Humus-rich topsoil forms a complex, chaotic ecosystem that has multiple ways of dealing with challenges. A healthy diverse ecosystem could be compared to a car owned by a good mechanic who works in a machine shop, reads car manuals in his spare time, and owns a comprehensive set of tools and spare parts. A simplified ecosystem—for instance, a chemically dependent garden—is like a car that is owned by a do-it-yourselfer who owns a hammer and a roll of duct tape and has lost his car's manual.

Medical researchers are finding that a little bit of chaos is far more healthy than none at all. They are learning to diagnose heart disease by the regularity of the heartbeat: the more regular the heartbeat, the less healthy the heart. Healthy hearts do not beat absolutely regularly because they are constantly adjusting to changing conditions inside and outside of the body. Diseased hearts are far less flexible and do not adjust to change quickly.

(continued)

> *A person with a healthy heart is like a vehicle with an automatic transmission with infinitely adjustable gears: the gears adjust accurately to the task at hand, putting the least possible strain on the engine. A person with a diseased heart is like a vehicle with a crotchety, worn-out clutch; the driver tends to avoid changing gears, thereby putting unnecessary strain on the engine.*

What's Your Soil Type?

If your garden soil is already good, you are extremely lucky. I have never begun a garden, whether for myself or for clients, which started with good soil.

The best undisturbed native soils in your area have the ideal amount of topsoil for your area. Because different climates produce different types of soil, it is useful to make some field trips to nearby natural areas in order to determine what kind of soil your climate produces.

In practice, this means going into a natural area near your home to find some undisturbed soil. For example, if you go to a nearby woods, brush aside the litter of leaves and twigs and probe around in the topsoil with a weeding tool or a twig until you reach the lighter-colored, less humusy soil layer underneath the topsoil. Topsoil depth will vary, but will tend to be deeper in areas of greater rainfall. If you find several inches of nice dark crumbly soil under the leaves, you can go ahead and build up your soil all you like, as long as you use well-composted materials.

If you live in the desert, you can probably gauge the depth of your native topsoil without bending over—topsoil formation is very slow to almost nonexistent in arid areas. Native plant and animal life is sparse in deserts, and organic material tends to dry up rather than decompose. This is why there are mummies in Egypt but not in England.

In an arid area, more than a light sprinkling of topsoil or compost may be too much. If you use landscaping plants that want rich, deep soil, they will also require a huge amount of water. If the soil in your area is naturally very thin, it is probably best to grow vegetables, which are very heavy feeders, in enclosed beds filled with composted manure.

After you have investigated some of the natural soils in your area, assess your own topsoil, if you have any. Topsoil is unlikely to exist under a nonporous surface like asphalt, concrete, or gravel-over-plastic. Topsoil can also be scarce where there has been new construction: the topsoil from new home sites is often dug up and sold by contractors.

Many plants thrive only under certain soil conditions. Whether the soil is rich or poor, alkaline or acidic, and whether it drains quickly or slowly are the questions the gardener needs to answer before beginning to plant. A very simple test can help answer a couple of these questions. Brush aside undecomposed material on the surface of your soil, then use a trowel to take a nine-inch-deep soil sample. Try to take a small, very uniform slice of the soil, so that the top inch of the sample has the same thickness as the bottom and middle of the sample. Find a clear glass jar big enough to hold the sample. Put the sample in the jar, and pour in enough water to cover the soil sample. Screw the jar lid on tightly, then shake the jar vigorously until all the soil is swirling around in the water. If some of the soil remains in a clump, wait an hour or so, then try shaking it again. Once all the soil has dissolved into the water, set the jar somewhere with good light where you won't have to move it for a day. After the soil has settled, you should be able to see distinct layers when you look at the jar. Gravel and stones fall the most quickly, and will be on the very bottom of the jar, sand settles next, then fine-grained silt, which is basically completely pulverized sand, and after quite awhile the clay, which is composed of miniscule particles of decomposed rock, will fall out of solution. The organic matter will be sitting uneasily on top, ready to swirl away at the slightest disturbance of the jar. Some organic material may still be floating in or on the water.

Use a measuring tape or ruler to measure the height of the soil in the jar, then measure each layer separately. You can calculate the makeup of your soil using these measurements. Ideally, soil should contain at least 10 percent humus, and between 20 and 30 percent clay. Soils that contain more than 35 percent clay are very heavy and tend to have poor drainage. Soils with less than 10 percent clay tend to dry out easily. Whether your soil is sandy or full of clay, compost is the remedy.

Many gardens contain more than one soil type. One soil sample may not be enough to give you the full picture of what kind of soil you are working with.

Many plants are adapted to life in very specific types of soil. Though you can improve clay soils and sandy soils by adding organic material, unless all the soil is removed and replaced, the underlying characteristics will remain. Clay soils are called heavy soils, and sandy soils are called light soils. Planting instructions for most plants specify whether the plant thrives in heavy or light soil, whether it needs good drainage or whether it likes wet feet, whether it prefers rich or poor soil.

Reputable nurseries give their customers clear and accurate information about the cultural requirements of the plants they are selling. Armed with this information, a gardener can design her garden to be as healthy as possible.

Soil acidity is closely tied to the amount of precipitation an area receives. Arid areas tend to have alkaline soil, while regions with high precipitation tend to have slightly acidic soil. Conveniently, many drought-tolerant plants are also tolerant of alkaline soils, and many thirsty plants tolerate slightly acidic soil. If you are choosing plants that are well adapted to your garden's conditions, pH tests are probably not necessary.

Soil Amendments Defined

I strongly believe that organic soil amendments should be made of renewable resources. Many agricultural and/or food processing by-products make wonderful additions to the soil once they are composted. Most parts of the country have some sort of organic by-products that are easily available to the home gardener.

Here are a few of my favorites:

COMPOST *is decayed organic material that improves soil texture, feeds soil microorganisms, increases the water-holding capacity of the soil, and makes plant nutrients more readily available to plants.*

COMPOSTED MANURE *is manure that has sat around in a pile for at least six months. Fully composted manure has no smell and is crumbly and fine-grained. Composted manure quickly turns to humus and becomes part of the topsoil.*

MULCH *is any loose material that is laid on top of the soil and not mixed in. Organic mulches such as shredded bark, cocoa bean hulls, rice hulls, grape pomace, straw, or leaves all eventually decompose and improve the soil. Inorganic mulches such as plastic sheeting or gravel do not improve the soil. All mulches help retain soil moisture, and all organic mulches tend to moderate soil temperatures.*

PEAT MOSS *is harvested from peat bogs. It is the dried and pulverized remains of aquatic moss that has sat around in water so cold that it prevents bacterial decomposition. Peat moss increases the soil's water-holding capacity as well as its acidity. Plants that need acidic soil should always have peat moss added to their planting holes.*

BONE MEAL *is generally made up of finely ground livestock bones. It is a by-product of beef processing. Bone meal is high in phosphorus and calcium and enhances flower production and fruit set. Many people put a dash of bone meal in the bottom of the hole when planting flower bulbs to increase the size of the blooms.*

(continued)

WOOD ASHES, *especially hardwood ashes, are a good source of potash and calcium and will decrease soil acidity. Ashes should be sprinkled over the ground very sparingly, especially if you are not adding compost to the soil.*

KELP, *the very large seaweed that grows in cold waters, stimulates the growth of beneficial soil microorganisms and adds trace minerals and potash to the soil. It is available commercially in liquid or powdered form.*

FISH EMULSION *is a filtered, stabilized product that is used as a general purpose fertilizer and is a good source of nitrogen. It is a by-product of the animal feed industry.*

NOTE : *I don't recommend the use of cottonseed meal, since cotton crops are commonly sprayed with large quantities of pesticides.*

Eliminate the Negative

Before you can begin the actual work of rebuilding your garden's soil, you need to clear out everything you don't want. If you are clearing out whiplike saplings, brambles, or shrubs, wear protective eyewear.

An abbreviated list of what I have had to remove before putting in a garden includes: sod, Bermuda grass, blackberry brambles, English ivy, stumps, shrubs, aloes, sapling trees, gravel, rotted plywood, asphalt, concrete, road dirt, and glass. Which reminds me: always don work gloves before sticking your hands into unfamiliar soil. If you have reason to believe that your soil is severely glass-infested, you might even want to buy a pair of cut-resistant gloves to wear under your work gloves. Slice-resistant gloves are commonly used in the meatpacking and seafood industries. They are sold through catalogue companies that sell protective clothing and safety equipment, and are either made of bulletproof fabric or stainless-steel chain links.

I really enjoy getting grimy and sweaty, and having the opportunity to hack or pull or push at things as hard as I can. But there is more than one way to skin a cat. (I had planned to cleverly interject here, in order to appease cat lovers, that skinning a cat refers to catfish; catfish have skin, not scales. Unfortunately, when I looked it up, I discovered that there is much disagreement as to whether the phrase refers to *Felis domestica;* a type of whip called the cat-o'-nine-tails; a catfish; or a gymnastic maneuver.) If you want to do the work yourself, but the prospect of a good hard tussle with something obstinate does not make your day, there are mechanized ways of doing almost any clearing job.

Clearing Ground

I. SOD. *If you are really in a hurry, sod can be dug out with a sod cutter; you can probably rent one at your nearest rental center. Sod can be composted by piling it upside down and covering it with compost, dirt, or black plastic to prevent it from starting to grow. If your sod is in good shape and you want to make new friends, roll up the sod and put a "free sod, U-haul" ad in the paper.*

If you are not in a hurry, sod is easy to smother by watering it thoroughly, covering it with black plastic sheeting, weighting the edges down with rocks or dirt, and letting it broil in the sun for a couple of months. Or you can compost your sod to death by burying it under six inches of composted manure or a foot or two of leaves. The sod will take a couple of months to die out and decompose.

2. GROUND COVERS. *Some ground covers—for example, ivy* (Hedera sp.), *crown vetch* (Coronilla varia), *and Japanese knotweed* (Polygonum cuspidatum)—*can be horribly persistent and difficult to eradicate. The best offense against overly vigorous ground covers is defense—ask around, then don't plant the truly invasive ones. If it is too*

(continued)

late for that, pull them out, dig them out, then smother them with several layers of cardboard topped with a thick, heavy layer of organic material. If you are the belt-and-suspenders type, you can top off the whole mess with a big compost pile.

3. ASPHALT OR CONCRETE SLABS. *Get out your pick, sledgehammer, and your big trusty pry bar (ours is about six feet long and weighs approximately seventy-five pounds). Put on safety goggles and work gloves. Jam the tip of the pry bar under the edge of the slab. Put a brick or piece of concrete under the pry bar so you can pry the slab up a bit and push the pry bar farther in. Then hit the slab directly over the pry bar with the sledgehammer until the slab cracks. Use the pick to pry up the pieces of slab. Don't try to break up asphalt if the weather is really hot; heat-softened asphalt bends but doesn't break. Or, rent a jackhammer and get some good ear protectors. Broken-up pieces of concrete can be used to make paths and "rock" walls; if you don't want them, try a "Free concrete pieces for paths or walls, U-haul" ad.*

Broken-up asphalt can be recycled into "hot mix" asphalt, or crushed and used in a gravel mix. Contact a local asphalt contractor or gravel pit to find out if they can use your asphalt.

4. GRAVEL BEDS. *Put a "free gravel, U-haul" ad in the paper.*

There may be some clearing chores you should not do yourself. For instance, if you are not skilled with a chain saw, and you need to get rid of large trees, I strongly recommend hiring a tree service. If you have a patch of poison oak or ivy, hiring a herd of goats to clear it out of your yard would be a very sensible thing to do.

Compost, Ambrosia of the Earth Goddess

Once you have rid your garden area of undesirables, you can start improving the soil. Adding large amounts of decomposed organic

material is really the only way to build up topsoil. Organic gardeners commonly add compost to their gardens every year from the
previous year's pile, but what does one do the first year? Answer:
one acquires a large amount of well-composted animal manure or
composted yard waste. When we moved to our new house, we
brought our compost pile with us. Compost is far too valuable to
abandon.

There are many materials that conventional wisdom
will advise you not to compost, among them meat scraps,
animal fats, and dairy products. While all these foods
will attract scavenging animals, if you are composting in
a mammal-proof building or container, there are very
few materials that are unsuitable for composting. Even pernicious weeds can be safely composted if you pretreat them
by letting them rot in a bucket of water until they turn
black. (Put a lid on the bucket so you don't provide a nursery for mosquito larvae.) This pre-rotting treatment kills all
parts of the weeds including the seeds, stems, roots, and
stolons. These pretreated, softened, blackened weeds are safe
to add to your compost pile.

Any clean, toxin-free organic material can be composted and
used safely in a garden. The following materials are not safe and
should *never* be composted for farming, gardening, or home landscape use: sawdust or shavings from chemically treated wood; wall-
board; plywood; tar paper; any materials that are contaminated
with pesticides, heavy metals, or petrochemicals; bleached papers
or paper printed with colored inks.

Composting human sewage and droppings from carnivorous
animals should be avoided by the home gardener—there is a danger of contracting intestinal parasites from these wastes, and human waste commonly contains heavy metals. Leave the composting
of these dangerous materials to the hazardous waste professionals.

Setting up a compost pile can be very simple or quite elaborate.
The simplest composting involves piling all the organic debris—
leaves, cuttings, rotten vegetables, and weeds—from your yard and

garden in an out-of-the-way area of your yard. Luckily, all organic material on our planet eventually decomposes, so after a few years your compost pile will be a pile of dirt. Build a new pile each year.

Compost piles need to have alternating layers of "green" and "brown" materials. In this context, green material is fresh plant material, which contributes nitrogen to the pile; brown material is dried plant material, which contributes carbon to the pile. The "classic" compost pile is constructed with three parts dry materials to one part fresh vegetable matter. Layer the green and brown materials as if you are making a sandwich. A base layer of sticks or branches laid on the ground will help keep the bottom of the pile aerated.

Many people sprinkle on lime or ashes from a fireplace or woodstove as they build their compost pile, especially if they are adding large amounts of acidic materials such as coffee grounds or apple pomace from cider making; the lime or ashes help neutralize the acid and speed up the composting process. But no matter what materials are composted, the finished product will be neutral to slightly alkaline. Composting is the great leveler.

Unless your green materials are extremely wet, you will need to water your compost pile thoroughly after you build it. A compost pile needs to be kept moist; covering it with a tarp, burlap sacks, or a layer of dirt or finished compost will help the pile retain its moisture. Water it if it dries out.

If you want a compost pile to work more quickly, you will need to put in a little more effort. Organic material breaks down more quickly in the presence of oxygen. There are two ways to oxygenate a compost pile: install pipes and blowers, or turn the pile. Depending on how much you enjoy playing with compost piles, you can turn your pile using a pitchfork, garden fork, shovel, or even your gloved hands, at intervals ranging from every other day to once per summer. Twin, triplet, or even quadruplet compost bins made of wire fencing or old wooden pallets can make turning a compost pile much simpler. When the compost needs to be turned, it can be forked from one bin into the neighboring bin. This is much easier than turning compost in a single bin.

I once visited a man who is phenomenally talented at composting. His paired compost bins were producing compost of the "chocolate cake" variety. He referred to putting kitchen scraps into his bins as "bringing offerings to the goddess."

I know exactly what he meant by that. The transformation of stinky, oozing garbage into the sweetest smelling material on earth is nothing short of miraculous. All living things on this planet are made up of elements that have cycled through the lifetimes of many different living beings.

I once fretted over the whereabouts of my "good" jeans for several cold months, until my compost pile thawed out in the spring, and I found them there, composting. I had forgotten that I had worn them out and thrown them in the pile the previous fall. Composting my old clothes gives me a satisfying feeling of continuity.

The Wisdom of Worms

I tend to compost in the least complicated way possible. I am simply not methodical enough to give a compost pile the care it needs to make it work quickly. But about ten years ago I figured out a way to compost that is pretty foolproof: every spring I put about a pound of my indoor vermicomposting worms in my compost pile. (Vermicomposting indoors in bins is a way that many of us who live in the northern intemperate zones avoid shoveling our way out to a frozen compost pile in midwinter.) My red wriggler worms (*Eisenia foetida*) are the descendants of the half cup of composting worms I ordered about fifteen years ago. They are such capable little composters that I don't have to do anything special to make my outdoor compost pile work. I just throw as much organic material on the pile as I can, and add a few pounds of worms every spring. The worms do all the aerating and mixing, bless their little quintuple hearts! Red wriggler worms can be mail-ordered through many gardening catalogues.

Edible Boots, Inedible French Fries

I have vermicomposted everything from a deer head that someone put in a school worm bin to let the worms clean off the flesh, to dryer lint, old clothes, dead mice, cracked natural rubber gloves (which took two years to break down), and old leather boots. Some things take longer than others to break down, but if it's organic, it will eventually capitulate.

Setting up vermicomposting systems in schools has been a composting revelation to me: our family doesn't eat many unhealthy foods, so without the help of a school lunch program, I would never have learned that 5 gallons of french fries when spread thinly across a 150-gallon worm bin would not only take nearly forever to break down but would meld into a fair imitation of a wet sheet of particle board: limp but intact. Where else but in a school would I have learned that corn dogs take months to decompose, that commercial cole slaw bubbles like a volcano even when refrigerated, or that pizza crusts coagulate into a sticky, stinky mass of doughy goo? Even the worms turn up their noses at these "foods." If you want to compost large amounts of processed foods, you will probably need a compost heap that is so big it will need to be turned using heavy equipment.

Research seems to show that decomposition helps neutralize

poisons. That bastion of liberal environmental ideals, the U.S. Department of Defense, has been evaluating techniques for treating hazardous munitions wastes since 1982. Composting and land farming are two of the methods being evaluated. So far, bacteria have been shown to degrade nitroaromatics, nitramines, nitrate esters, petroleum-based hydrocarbons, pentachlorophenol, and polycyclic aromatic hydrocarbons. Apparently, compost can even save the day for the Defense Department.

Cheap as Dirt

Let us assume that your garden site has little or no topsoil. First, you need to decide how much money you are willing to spend to get it.

If you have time but not money, topsoil will take longer to build up, but a few years of work can produce wonderful soil. Unless you own livestock, one of the cheapest ways to add organic material to your soil is to grow green manures. Green manures are crops which produce a large amount of green material in a single season. The crop is cut before it sets seed, then it's allowed to rot in place or is tilled into the soil; the plot can be gardened or farmed the following year. Though farmers traditionally use clover, alfalfa, buckwheat, grasses, soybeans, field beans, and vetch for their green manures, just about any annual or biennial plant can be planted thickly to be used as a green manure. A bed of green manure doesn't have to be boring: a thickly planted bed of flowering kale will produce an enormous quantity of organic matter, and a crop of sweet peas is just as beneficial to your soil as a crop of field peas. If you choose a plant in the cabbage family as your green manure, you may want to either till it in thoroughly or bury it well under a foot or two of autumn leaves—many people are not fond of the smell of rotting cabbages.

If you want a quicker start, you may want to begin scrounging for organic material that you can either layer all over your garden beds for "sheet composting" or use to build a compost pile. Either way, it is nearly impossible to have too much organic material. A few strategically placed "Leaves wanted" signs may help, as will driving through neighborhoods in the autumn and snagging bags of leaves that are left at the curb. I strongly recommend asking permission before appropriating bagged leaves, especially those which are not set by garbage cans or on the curb. The lust for more and more compostable materials has driven many an otherwise respectable organic gardener to a life of petty leaf-snatching in the autumn.

Because sheet composting occurs right on the garden beds, you will need to be a little more picky about your raw materials. It is often possible to get old horse or cow manure for very little money. If fresh manure is all you can get, it will need to be composted under deep layers of leaves in order to filter out the smell. By the following year, all these compostables will have turned to beautiful soil, ready to be planted into. Sheet composting is a great time saver at this point, since all the soil will already be in place.

If you have more money than time, or you are landscaping for a client, improving the soil becomes quite easy; you hunt down a source of well-composted cattle manure which has been screened to remove rocks, sticks, and trash. Ask gardeners in your area to recommend the source for the best compost. Sometimes this compost is called "black dirt," sometimes it is called "garden soil," sometimes it is called "mushroom compost." (Mushroom compost is composted, sterilized manure that was used to grow mushrooms.) Whatever it is called, it should be "like chocolate cake." Order enough of it to make at least a six-inch layer everywhere you will be gardening.

Well-composted cattle or sheep manure can also be bought in bags at many hardware stores and garden centers. Though bagged compost is fine stuff, it can be rather expensive if you need a large amount.

Now comes the really fun part. You have your big pile of luscious dirt and your cleared garden beds are anxiously awaiting it. If your garden beds are dry, water them thoroughly before you begin shoveling compost. Once you have dumped enough compost in the beds, rake it level. Next, start tamping the compost down, either by rolling it with a lawn roller (can be found at rental centers); by putting down old sheets of plywood, then walking all over the plywood; or, if the bed is really small, simply tramp over every square inch of it.

If you don't compress the composted manure, it will add fertility to your soil, but it will perform like a mulch, not like topsoil. Tamping the compost down squeezes out some of its air and helps connect it to the ground underneath. The tamped-down compost then functions as the top layer of the soil, and moisture can wick into it from underneath. If you have forgotten to dampen the ground before starting to tamp down the soil, you may find that the compost is lifting off the dry soil and sticking to the lawn roller. If the roller is pulling compost up off the ground, soak the whole area thoroughly, then try tamping it down the next day after the surface has dried slightly.

Once your six-inch layer of compost has been squeezed down to about two inches, your garden is ready to be planted. That was easy, wasn't it?

"What, No Rototilling?"

We have never tilled any of our gardens. Rototilling kills worms and destroys the soil's structure, preventing the "wicking action" that helps plants survive drought. Tilling also pushes large amounts of absorbent material below the root zones of many plants. This buried organic material can act like a sponge, soaking up water and preventing it from reaching the root zone.

We once took over a friend's landscape maintenance job for the summer while he went on vacation. The landscape was newly installed, and before he left, our friend informed us that he was worried about the health of some coyote brushes he had planted—they didn't look healthy to him. When we went to the job, the coyote brushes (*Baccharis pilularis*) were looking slightly brownish (the plant equivalent of queasy), and languishing in their nicely mulched bed. I had just been reading about soil wicking, the capillary action that brings soil moisture from lower levels up to where plants' roots can reach it. Just for fun, I gently stepped on a coyote brush; the soil was so fluffed up from rototilling that my weight pushed the plant down considerably. Realizing that the plants might be languishing from thirst, I gently stepped on all the plants, then trod down the whole bed. The bushes looked better and better on each of our successive visits.

Though coyote brush is one of the weediest, toughest, meanest "landscaping specimens" one could ever hope to plant in California, these particular specimens had been dying of thirst in their fluffy bed. Air pockets beneath the plants were preventing soil moisture from getting to the roots. Stepping on these plants was the nicest thing I could have done for them.

Mother Nature's Soil Recipe

Mother Nature likes her soil layered, not stirred. So do I.

Under natural circumstances, soil is built from the top down as organic material decomposes on the surface and is gradually incorporated into the soil by worms, insects, and other animals. Soil is made up of layers, with a loose mulch of dead plant and animal material in various stages of decomposition on the surface and, beneath that, a layer of humus-rich topsoil. Beneath that the soil gradually decreases in humus content. The deepest soil level is the humus-free subsoil, with the bedrock lurking just below.

In Nature, when the subsoil is on top, it is because a landslide, mudflow, flood, volcano, or other natural disaster has occurred. Soil-churning disasters activate Mother Nature's emergency soldiers: tough, deep-rooted weeds that help hold the soil against erosion and begin the arduous task of soil reconstruction. Many of these weeds have seeds that can lie dormant in the soil for extremely long periods of time. Rototilling can unearth these dormant seeds and allow them to germinate. Nature has equipped her "Natural Guard" troops with many strategies to help them survive; some of these plants, like lupines, are just plain tough. Others are not quite as pretty or benign as lupines. I believe in letting sleeping weeds lie.

Chapter Four

Raising a Well-Adjusted GARDEN

 ardening can be done quickly, expensively,
and intrusively: moving mature trees with large
equipment, turning hills into valleys, valleys into
hills, digging lakes, filling lakes, making the high
low and the low high. This is not a new approach to
landscaping—in the seventeenth century, the French leveled hills
to produce a flat garden, while seventeenth-century Persians did
the reverse.

There are two basic approaches to financing a landscape. The
first is the more-money-than-time landscape, which is also known
as the "we're having a wedding here in two months" garden. To
ready the garden for the wedding, one needs to buy a load of well-
composted, screened manure; hire help; buy enough plants to fill
the area in question; spread the compost; install the plants; cover
all the bare soil with a dark mulch such as cocoa bean hulls, and
voilà! (or, as our son says, viola!) the wedding garden is ready. The
second is the more-time-than-money approach, in which the gardener will need to substitute time, energy, and ingenuity for cash.
Rather than ordering a load of expensive topsoil, the gardener
may need to improve his own soil by composting cheap or free organic materials; plant materials may need to be started from cuttings, divisions, and seeds; and paths may be paved with blocks
made of broken-up concrete, used bricks, wood chips, crushed

seashells, or other cheap or free materials. Both the more-money-than-time and the more-time-than-money methods of garden building can be a lot of fun.

Using Your Mind's Eye

Close your eyes and imagine a tiny, walled garden in a big city, with brick paths, clipped box hedges, a smog-tolerant tree, and a tiny handkerchief lawn. Now visualize a climbing rose rambling up the tree, blooming in your favorite color. This is the essence of landscaping: you look at what is there, and imagine what could be there. The more local gardens and nurseries you visit, the more efficient your imagination will become, and the better your fantasies will mesh with reality. Eventually, if you are lucky, your garden dreams will feature plants that are well adapted to your area.

Planting Protocols

1. *Enrich soil from the surface*
2. *Choose healthy, hardy plants*
3. *Give plants the cultural conditions they need in order to thrive*
4. *Pay attention to the eventual size of plants. Most perennials can be moved easily, but trees and shrubs are much more difficult to move*
5. *Plant good neighbors that need the same cultural conditions*
6. *Plan for succession, allow the garden to change as its conditions change*

Luckily for all of us, healthy plants are much more beautiful than any human hand could ever make them. Their very presence can transform even the most simple gardens into places of overwhelming loveliness. As they say, if you haven't got your health, you haven't got anything. This is even more so for a garden. A healthy garden builds up an enormous amount of momentum and tends to keep itself going, while an unhealthy garden has no momentum of its own, and needs continual encouragement.

Accentuate the Positive

Before you begin gardening, it is a good idea to inventory what you have, and decide which features you like and which you do not. Your landscape may contain some features you like and want to keep, as well as some features you dislike and want to get rid of. Existing garden assets may include old trees or other valuable plant specimens, large rocks, good soil, interesting outbuildings, productive fruit trees or bushes, wildlife habitat, good sun exposure, ponds, or streams.

Often you need to clear things out before you can begin landscaping. *But!* Removing a native tree which is a couple of hundred years old because you want more sun is not acceptable, and in some areas not legal. If a venerable tree is getting in your way, buy a different house.

Even if you don't plan to cut down a valuable native specimen, you may not be prepared to care for it appropriately. Many native plants require very different care than do garden cultivars; some natives can be killed by common gardening practices. I implore you, if you "own" an old native tree, look up its cultural requirements and try to accommodate them. Your county extension agent can also be a valuable source of information.

Many native trees are quite sensitive to change. For example, paper birches need their ground-covering friends under them; if the area under an old birch is mowed or cleared, the tree may die. Many different hardwood species resent having their root zones stepped on or disturbed. Oaks are particularly delicate. California live oaks cannot tolerate changes in the ground level anywhere near them; their roots must be buried at exactly the same level at all times. Grading nearby to build a house, or putting an extra inch of dirt over their roots can kill them. These magnificent trees can also be killed by summer irrigation, and since their roots extend far out beyond the drip line, the "Do Not Disturb" zone around a mature tree is rather large.

When I was very young, my best friend's father wanted to cut down the live oak in front of their house. The tree was ancient, its trunk was the size of a small room, but it had seen better days. Nearby street grading had sickened it, and many of its limbs had rotted and been cut off. My friend's father was informed by his wife that he'd have to cut the tree down over her dead body.

Many years later, the old oak was still living, but tragically, its far more robust brother across the street was gone; the man who moved into the house under that tree wanted more sun, and had the tree cut down. All the neighbors refused to speak to him for ten years.

Making Silk Flowers Out of Sows' Ears, or, Even Ugly Features Are Better Than None

It is often easier to landscape around existing features, no matter how ugly, than to deal with a blank slate. Sometimes a garden can coalesce around an irritation, such as an ugly well or wall, like a pearl around a grain of sand. If you have to hide an ugly wall, a neighbor's fence, a vent pipe, a shed, a garage, or a propane tank, there is suddenly purpose behind your landscaping, and things begin to fall into place.

If you are really lucky, your garden features something that you like: a fence, a huge rock, a hill, a beautiful old lilac bush. Working around the bones of an old landscape can produce a truly magnificent new landscape.

Sometimes the defining features of a garden are not immediately apparent. Underground features such as drainage patterns, springs, seeps, changing soil types, and buried boulders sometimes determine the conditions above them. Working with, not against these elements, can give your garden its own personality and charm.

The soil may dry out rapidly above a buried boulder, making it an ideal spot to plant herbs or cacti or to install an alpine rock garden. If a seep at the corner of your yard is drowning your lawn, plant bog iris or dig a small pond.

Last spring, as I was patrolling our potholes, pouring a drop of vegetable oil into each one to prevent mosquitoes, I stumbled across a low spot, and thought it might be a good location for a small pond. A previous owner had thought it was a wonderful spot for a junk pile. As I was moving bedsprings and rusted-out buckets and the bumpers and fenders of an old car, I realized that every likely spot in our yard had already been used for something else by previous owners. I think pond; they thought dump. I think greenhouse; they thought ash pile. I think raspberry patch; they thought chicken coop.

The land whispers: "Here, right here, is the perfect spot for …" We just fill in the blanks.

Size Matters

Trees are wonderful, but there is nothing wrong with cutting down a tree that really doesn't belong. Our first Christmas tree was a young Atlas cedar that we harvested (with permission) from a client's front yard. The previous owner had planted the tree about six feet from the house, and mature Atlas cedars can grow to be sixty feet across. The house was only about twenty-five feet deep—if the tree had been allowed to grow to maturity, it might have ended up in front *and* in back of the house.

When you are designing your garden, pay close attention to the maximum size plants can reach. Though pruning done for aesthetic purposes can enhance the appearance of many plants, pruning done for purely practical purposes can be less than aesthetically pleasing; trees lopped off to accommodate power lines are a particularly sad sight; a tree planted too close to a house will either suffer or make the house suffer; and shrubs or bushes planted too close to a walkway will eventually either have to be drastically pruned or removed.

Plant sizes can sometimes differ considerably under different conditions. Though Monterey pines (*Pinus radiata*) are rather picturesque, wind-gnarled, smallish trees in their native seaside habitat, when they are planted inland, away from ocean winds and salt sprays, they are extremely fast growers which, by age twelve, can grow to fifty feet, half their mature height. Homeowners who have paid dearly for panoramic views often do not appreciate it when their neighbors plant such fast-growing trees.

Miscalculating the eventual size of annuals, perennials, or vegetables is a much less serious problem than miscalculating trees, and can be rather amusing. When we moved farther inland from Lake Superior, and away from the cool, foggy "lake effect," I was astonished at the size of my inland vegetable plants, which were ten times as big as I was expecting. My tomato plants broke their fences, the bean plants snapped off their poles, the rutabagas were the size of a baby's head, the chard was knee high, and the winter squashes overwhelmed half the garden. Though all my careful vegetable planning went for naught, the effect was giddying. Squash plants have now been banished to the compost pile, which they adore anyway.

*" From each according to his abilities, to each according
to his needs."*
—KARL MARX

Communism may not be an efficient way to run an economy,
but it is the only healthy way to run a garden.

Compared to animals, which must ingest food regularly in order to survive, plants are fairly self-sufficient. Sunlight shining on
leaves powers photosynthesis, which converts carbon dioxide and
water into sugar. Roots seek out and absorb water and dissolved
nutrients that are used to manufacture proteins, oils, hormones, vitamins, and other compounds necessary for healthy plant growth.

The best thing we can do to help leaves do their job is to give
them the amount of sunlight they need. If you try planting sun-
loving plants on the north side of your house, they will be unhappy,
and you will be disappointed.

Most plants' roots require soil that contains both water and oxygen. The structure of healthy soils can generally provide roots with
what they need, but soils differ, as do plants. Remember that
plants, like people, thrive best in congenial surroundings—some of
us require a lot of water, and some of us don't. Cacti and bog iris
do not make good bedfellows. One or the other is bound to suffer
from the cultural conditions in their bed.

It isn't a bad idea to make a water map of your property, show-
ing which areas are wet and which are dry, before you begin to design your garden. The vegetation that is growing in different areas
can help you figure out your garden's moisture zones. For example,
horsetails are a sign of wet soil, as are cattails and alders; hawkweed is a sign of very dry soil. There is an excellent little book
called *Weeds and What They Tell*, by Ehrenfried E. Pfeiffer, which de-
scribes many common weedy plants and the soil conditions— wet
or dry, rich or poor, acidic or alkaline—that favor them. Reading
this book will help you learn to "read" your soil, which can be a
very interesting and useful pastime.

Plants that are well adapted to your climate will require far less coddling, and use up far fewer resources than ill-adapted plants will. We all owe it to our beautiful but finite planet to work within our climate's limitations— the results will also be far more satisfactory.

The amount of feeding that plants need also varies widely: what spoils one may be just what another needs. Some plants, roses for instance, are very heavy feeders; it is almost impossible to give

them too much nitrogen. But others, nasturtiums for example, bloom best in the poorest soil; nitrogen-rich soil makes them produce a lot of lush leaves and nothing else. But whether you are feeding gluttonous plants or light feeders, it is always better to fertilize more lightly and more often, rather than heavily and infrequently, so the fertilizer can be absorbed by the soil and used by the plants in your garden, not by the algae in waterways.

Raising fruit trees is very similar to raising children: saplings, like babies, need to be very well taken care of. It isn't possible to spoil a baby. Young trees need to be fed regularly, watered deeply, and carefully pruned for the first few years after they are planted, in order to become strong and healthy enough to support later fruit production. But after those crucial first few years, fruit trees should be fed far more sparingly. Overfed trees, like spoiled children, are underproductive and slow to mature. Heavily fed fruit trees keep growing rapidly, producing more tree, not more fruit.

Overfeeding young trees (or young humans) can lead to disease; for example, young Bartlett pear trees are very susceptible to fireblight if their nitrogen levels are too high. Letting grass grow under these trees helps reduce the succulence of the twigs and helps prevent the bacterial infection. Mature trees generally don't need to be fertilized at all. Their root systems are so large that they can fend for themselves.

Artemisia and Old Maize: Are Your Plants Poisoning Each Other?

Congenial neighbors are a great blessing. But for plants, having good neighbors can be a matter of life and death. Successful botanical matchmaking requires more than simply finding plants that share similar tastes in food, water, and soil types. It is quite similar to trying to come up with the perfect seating arrangement for a large, argumentative family at a wedding. If you don't want casualties, you'd better not sit Auntie Rue next to Cousin Basil at the dinner table or in the vegetable garden.

Some plants are generally friendly and gregarious, while others are the botanical equivalents of hermits. Some unsociable plants out-compete other plants by monopolizing more than their share of sunshine, water, or nutrients. Others produce chemicals that inhibit or kill other plants. These biochemical effects, which modern scientists have dubbed "allelopathy," have been noticed by farmers and gardeners for millennia.

In the first century B.C., the Roman agricultural writer Varro observed that black walnut trees make the soil near them sterile, and black walnut trees remain the most infamous of the allelopathic plants. Walnut leaves, nut hulls, and roots all exude a potent chemical that inhibits the respiration of most other plant species. Tomatoes, peppers, and eggplants are particularly sensitive to walnut-induced suffocation.

Many plants produce chemicals that affect other plants. Scientists have only systematically studied these chemicals since the mid-twentieth century, and very few plant interactions have been researched so far. More is unknown than is known about allelopathy, so the observations made by gardeners are quite valuable. If you notice that a plant is looking a bit peaked—stunted, yellowing, or wilting—try moving it to another location. If the ailing plant perks up after it is moved, one of its old neighbors may have been poisoning it. If you take good notes, you can keep track of these interactions, and eventually solve the mystery of who attacked whom.

The following plants have been documented as being allelopathic:

TREE-OF-HEAVEN *(Ailanthus)*, eucalyptus, and black walnut trees all inhibit the growth of most other plants. Sycamores and hackberries are slightly less toxic; they inhibit the growth of nonwoody plants but don't bother other trees.

SHRUBS that are known to be allelopathic include manzanita, which inhibits grasses; laurel, which inhibits spruce; and rhododendron and sumac, which inhibit Douglas fir.

MANY GRASSES are hostile to other plants. For example, fescue stunts the roots of young trees, sorghum roots release a powerful weed suppressant, and rye and quack grass cuttings release chemicals that inhibit other plants.

OILY, STRONGLY AROMATIC PLANTS are more likely than less pungent plants to be toxic to other species. Some herbs such as sage, rue, and tansy strongly inhibit the growth of most nearby plants. These hostile botanicals should be planted in a far corner of the garden and given plenty of room. A plant that is surrounded by a ring of barren ground is likely to be poisoning its neighbors. Hostile plants, like hostile people, eventually end up alone.

Sunflowers are so hostile to other plants that pole beans refuse to climb them. Sunflower hulls can be an extremely effective herbicide. The built-up piles under your bird feeder are a valuable resource. Sweep sunflower hulls into the cracks between paving stones to prevent weeds from germinating. Sunflower hulls take a long time to break down. Your walkways should remain weed-free for at least one gardening season. If you want a neater look, grind the hulls up in an old blender or coffee grinder, then pour the herbicidal sludge or dust into the cracks in your sidewalk. An old blender that is used solely for the production of homemade garden products can be a very useful gardening tool.

Some plants are selectively hostile. Roses thrive in the company of garlic and chives: underplanting rosebushes with garlic or chives makes the flowers more fragrant, and the pungent smell of the chives and garlic also helps repel aphids. Peas and beans, however, are severely stunted by the presence of any member of the onion family.

You can accomplish a lot by manipulating plant materials intelligently. Think of yourself as the general of the garden. Scientists have discovered that the allelopathic properties of plants are strongest when the plant material is fresh, and the toxicity diminishes as plant material decomposes. Fresh grass clippings, scented leaves, alfalfa hay, and the fallen leaves from walnut, *Ailanthus,* eucalyptus, or other strong-smelling plants can all inhibit plant growth. Fresh wood chips or uncomposted bark—especially from walnuts, redwoods, eucalyptus, or cedars—are also extremely hostile. If you are trying to prevent weed growth, a fresh mulch of any of these materials will do the job.

Unless you are trying to produce compost that prevents plants from growing, do not put walnut leaves in your main compost pile. Compost them in a separate pile, and let the pile rot for several years before you even think about using it.

Clearing the Water

Decomposing barley straw slows the growth of algae in ponds and lakes. Commercial barley straw products are on the market, but if you can find barley straw, a homemade algae-prevention device can be made by putting loose barley straw in plastic-netting onion or orange bags, along with air-filled plastic bottles to act as floats. The filled bags should be suspended in the upper three or four feet of the pond. It takes about a pound of barley straw per one hundred square feet of water surface to help keep a pond clear.

Cultivating Friends

Eventually, if their plants are happily situated, most gardeners end up with more plants than their gardens can accommodate. Luckily for gardeners, surplus garden plants are far easier to resettle than are excess puppies and kittens. (Please, unless you own valuable show animals, have your pets spayed and neutered. A stray geranium left to die on a compost heap is far less tragic than a stray kitten staggering alongside a road.) If your friends can't use all your plants' progeny, placing a "Free garden perennials" advertisement in the newspaper may enlarge your circle of friends.

Everyone has heard of gardeners leaving loads of zucchini on neighbors' doorsteps, but there are also gardeners who give away enough plants to replant their own gardens many times over. Gardeners who wouldn't dream of giving money to a stranger will happily give dozens of beautiful plants to that same person. Many gardeners tell me they always remember who gave them a particular plant, and every time they go into the garden, they think about that person. I wish I could claim the same, but my memory is so pathetic that I generally can't remember what I ate for breakfast. The bounty of the natural world enables us all to be more generous. The wonderful thing about giving away plants is that the original garden can end up healthier for being thinned, the recipient is thrilled with the new plants, and the donor is given an opportunity to be generous.

Very nice gardens can be built around cuttings, seeds, and plants donated by friends. These gift gardens tend to be extremely hardy, since plants that aren't perfectly adapted to local conditions don't grow, spread, and reproduce well enough to be given away.

Getting Down to the Nitty-gritty

It is easiest to begin a new landscape with plants rather than by starting from seed. Though annuals tend to be rather easy to start from seed, I find that if I put annual plants, rather than seeds, in the garden, I not only have better luck the first year, but in subsequent years some annuals naturalize, and establish themselves as "weeds." Perennials can be more difficult to start from seed, yet many perennials that are finicky in a seeding flat will seed themselves with abandon in the garden. I will never be as good at multiplying plants as the plants are themselves, just as I will never be as good at composting as my worms are. Much of my gardening knowledge involves knowing when to get out of the way.

The best time to plant and transplant is when it is cool and overcast. Keep the plant in the shade until you plant it; roots are quickly damaged by the sun's rays. When I need to plant on a sunny day, I try to keep my back to the sun, with the plant in my shade. As soon as the plant is in its planting hole, you can carefully step on the soil around the plant to press out air pockets and connect the plant to its new home. This maneuver resembles a very gentle version of the Mexican hat dance: don't ever step on the crown. Water the transplant in thoroughly but gently, using either a fine mist spray from a hose or a watering can with a very fine rose so you don't wash the soil around, until all its soil turns to mud. If the plant sinks, you can grasp it by the stem and gently pull it up until it is sitting at the right level. You will have to gently poke the muddy soil with your finger or a tool handle to get rid of air pockets after raising the level of a plant in this way. A couple of days of shade, provided by some wisps of straw or a few leafy twigs will help the transplant adapt to its new location. A very small plant can be dug up with so much soil that it won't even realize it was moved.

If your soil is very dry, it is a good idea to water your intended planting area as well as the plants you will be moving the day before you plan to do your transplanting. This will give the soil time to soften up yet quit being muddy before you begin to dig.

If you are transplanting a lot of plants, it is a good idea to have buckets, flats, or bushel baskets with some damp soil in them in readiness for plants that have left their soil behind.

The more varied your plantings, the healthier they will be. If a pest must use up too much energy traveling from plant to plant, it will seek food elsewhere. Insect pests are attracted to chemicals released by their favorite foods. Large plantings of a single plant send out powerful, undiluted chemical messages that pests respond to in the same way hungry people respond to the food smells emanating from restaurants. If the food smells were mixed with perfume, we might be less likely to go into the restaurant.

Don't Upset Your Soil

Plants, especially trees, need to be planted in soil that approximates the real conditions of the site, not in an "enriched" hole. If a planting hole is filled in with soil that is richer than the surrounding soil, its roots will tend to circle around and around in the rich soil, and never "leave home." The circling roots will eventually strangle the plant.

I try to avoid disturbing the soil unless I am digging a planting hole or regrading the soil. When I have to disturb the soil, I try to replace the soil layers in their original order. In practice this means that when I dig a hole, I make separate piles for separate dirt layers. Every time the color or texture of the soil changes, I make a new pile. When I have finished digging the hole and planted the plant, or put in the pipe, or whatever I'm doing, I backfill the hole by replacing the soil in its correct order. When I am done, the soil in the hole is richest at the top, and poorest at the bottom. I then tread the soil down to remove air pockets, and the soil is not too much the worse for wear.

Tree Planting

Planting trees is similar to planting smaller plants, but more strenuous.

Before you begin digging a planting hole, you need to remove any sod or weeds that will get in your way. Using a shovel to cut through the sod, make a circle a little bigger than the hole you are planning to dig, then use the shovel to slice under the sod as if you were lifting a piece of pie out of a pie tin with a spatula. Compost the sod you have removed somewhere else.

Put a tarp down before you begin digging, and dump your shovel loads of dirt on the tarp. This will make clean-up much easier. Make separate piles for topsoil and the soil underneath, and start a new pile every time the color or texture of the soil changes. This will enable you to put the soil layers back in the correct order.

Trees are sold either bare-root, balled and burlapped, or in pots. Bare-root plants have been grown in the ground, rather than in pots, and are dug out; divested of most of their soil; packed in damp moss, sawdust, or excelsior; then wrapped with plastic. This makes them lighter and easier to transport than if they were moved along with a large amount of soil. The potted trees one can buy in nurseries are often bare-root trees that were potted up at the nursery.

The planting hole for a bare-root tree should be only slightly larger than the diameter of the root mass and just deep enough that the tree will stand at the same level in its new planting hole as it did in its old one.

Planting a tree slightly higher than it stood before is preferable to planting it lower—root bark can adapt to being exposed to the air, but trunk bark will rot if it is buried. If you examine the tree's trunk carefully, you should be able to see the planting level, where root bark meets trunk bark; you might want to use chalk to mark the trunk at the junction of root and trunk bark.

When the hole is finished, rough up its sides and bottom with a cultivator or garden fork to eliminate any shininess caused by the polishing action of the shovel, which might make the hole too watertight.

A bare-root tree should be kept in a cool, dark place until you are ready to plant it, and then soaked in water until the instant you lower it into the hole. Whenever possible, choose a cool day for transplanting, and don't let any sun shine on the roots. Any part of the root that has been broken or damaged should be pruned off before the tree is planted. The roots should be gently and carefully spread out in the hole, and none should be permitted to curl around, lest they continue in that direction as they grow and eventually strangle the plant. It is far better to shorten a root than to let it start to circle.

Shovel some of the dirt from the bottom level of the hole back into the hole to make a conical pile of dirt to support the roots, so the tree will sit in the hole with its bark junction slightly higher than ground level. Arrange the roots over the cone so they point away from the trunk and don't cross each other. Filling in the planting hole is much easier if one person holds the tree upright while the other fills the hole with dirt.

Fill the hole in with dirt in the same order in which it was removed: poorest soil on the bottom, getting gradually richer on the way up. Really horrible soil and rocks can be left out of the hole entirely, since the root ball will take up some space. Remember, soil is built from the top down. Don't mix rich soil into your planting hole, use compost only as a final mulch.

As you backfill, work the soil into the roots using your (gloved) fingers. The person holding the tree can also gently shake the trunk while the hole is being filled to help the soil settle. The tree holder should be very careful to keep the tree sitting high enough in its hole; a board set across the hole can be used to check the level of the hole against the desired soil level that you have marked on the tree trunk. Once the roots are covered with a couple of inches of soil, you can tamp it down by gently stepping on the soil. All of these prodding, shaking, and tamping activities help eliminate air pockets.

If you are planting a potted tree, dig the hole just wide enough to hold the plant. The soil level of the planted tree should be the same as it was in the pot. A potted tree is comparatively simple to plant. If you are having difficulty removing the tree from its pot, don't force it: cut the pot open with shears (if it is a metal pot, wear heavy leather gloves to do this). Remove the tree from its pot and examine its root ball; circling roots must either be straightened out or trimmed off with a sharp knife or pruner. If roots completely filled the pot, dig in with your fingers and gently rip the roots apart, or if you are confronted with a very pot-bound, solid mass of roots, use a sharp knife to make a quarter-inch-deep cut down all four sides, and a one-quarter-inch-deep cross on the bottom of the root ball. Once the unpotted plant is in its planting hole, pack garden soil in the gap between the root ball and the sides of the hole. From here on, planting care is the same as for bare-root trees.

Continue filling the hole with progressively richer soil, and tamping it down with your feet until the hole is full. Then water the tree until the soil turns to mud, and gently shake the trunk again to try to work out any remaining pockets of air. Then you can mulch with a couple of inches of composted manure over the bare soil, keeping it away from the trunk. If water is running away from the tree, you can build a little mound at the edge of the planting hole to hold in the water.

Leave No Ground Bare

Unlike point source pollution, which pours out of industrial waste pipes, non–point source pollution is difficult to trace to its origin. We are all responsible for non–point source pollution, which largely consists of polluted runoff from pavement or bare ground, which can contaminate surface and groundwater. Every time your car leaks oil onto pavement, or mud runs off your garden and into the street, you are contributing to non–point source pollution. The way we garden can have a large impact on the health of our local waterways. Vegetated land absorbs water efficiently, but when the land is plowed it loses much of its water-holding capacity, and non-porous paving absorbs no water at all.

I cannot do too much about runoff from our township road, but I can landscape so there is no runoff from my garden. Increasing the humus content of the soil, covering bare ground with mulch and vegetation, and minimizing paving are all very effective methods for reducing runoff. After so many years of gardening, the sight of bare ground makes my teeth ache; it's like looking at a skinned animal.

About ten years ago we bought a small house that had asphalt sloping all the way down from the back alley, across the parking pad, which took up half the yard, then down to the rear foundation wall. The owners had wondered why the basement flooded every time it rained, no matter how light the rain.

I spent a whole summer breaking up asphalt with a pick, sledgehammer, and crowbar, much to the amusement of the neighbors. At the edge of the parking pad there was an ash sapling, just about my height. Once the ground around it was freed of asphalt, we dug the little tree up and transplanted it to the edge of the yard.

After we leveled the yard, we got a load of compost, spread it where the asphalt had been, and planted a grass and clover mixture. We had a tough, thriving lawn within three months. The little tree is now large enough for a child to climb, and the basement stays dry when it rains.

Garden to Please Yourself, Not Your Neighbor

The drive to acquire new and different plant materials is a very old and deeply ingrained one, reaching at least as far back as ancient Egypt. It reached the pinnacle of absurdity in seventeenth-century Holland, where the hottest commodity was tulips. An illicit trade in tulip bulbs sprang up, fueled by the desire of rich plant collectors to own the most beautiful, rare, and expensive tulips available. Huge fortunes were made by merchants catering to the tulip mania of the rich. The prospect of easy money soon lured investors into selling the farm, the family jewels, and anything else that wasn't nailed down, and investing in tulips. The bottom fell out of the tulip market in 1637, and many Dutch families were ruined.

New plant varieties are often offered for very high prices in catalogues. If you can wait a few years to acquire your tartan rose, blue-and-green paisley tomatoes, or snapdragon that whistles "Dixie," you should be able to acquire a specimen for a fraction of what it would have cost the first year it was released.

Last summer I planted an annual called "Shoofly," which is a member of the tomato family. I had never seen it before, but it sounded interesting: the plant is supposed to repel insects and produces sky-blue flowers. The plants attained shrub size amazingly quickly, but when they began to bloom, the pretty blue flowers were so insignificant compared to the amount of leaf area that I ended up ripping the plants out while they were in bloom.

The shoofly taught me that the old standby annuals are garden classics because they work so well: they grow easily, have long blooming seasons, and produce a large amount of bloom relative to their leaf area. Classic plants—for example, alyssum, violas, lilacs, and sweet peas—are classics because they are pretty and smell wonderful, not because they are boring.

Vive la Différence!

When you are planning your paradise, bear in mind that unless you are God, paradise does not happen instantly. Nature begins with tough, hardy plants, many of which we call "weeds," that thrive in unbalanced ecosystems. These plants build up the soil and hold it in place, "unpaving" the way for less tough plants to follow. We can emulate this natural succession in our own gardens by planting sun-loving annuals and biennials or even fields of wild-flowers in our new gardens and gradually replacing them with perennials, shrubs, and trees.

Eventually a rich and well-balanced system can develop in which the resident plants and animals thrive and reproduce. This is where a lot of homeowners make mistakes—they don't realize that a garden is a living system that grows and changes over time. If you are doing a good job, the garden will incline toward more richness and diversity, and the soil will be more complex than when you started. If you are not doing a good job, there will be less diversity, the soil will become impoverished, and the tougher, more aggressive weeds will move in.

Sometimes, if you are having real trouble getting plants to grow in an area, it is a good idea to let nature take its course. If the only thing that will grow in that northwest corner is poplars, let them grow there. Eventually the poplars will build up the soil, and other plants will be able to grow there too.

There are many ways to encourage diversity. I have passed quite a few houses with tiny front yards whose handkerchief-size lawns sport one or two patches of gaily blooming weeds like orange hawkweed, oxeye daisies, bellflower, or purple asters, which have been carefully mown around.

If you can get together with your neighbors and let contiguous areas of your yards be "wild," you can create valuable habitat for wildlife as well as play spaces for juvenile humans.

Last spring I toured a garden that has been astonishingly transformed by its owner. When she bought the house, the landscape consisted of a large lawn with a few flowering shrubs scattered in small planting beds.  Through judicious use of a sod cutter, scavenged soil from neighborhood construction sites, and serendipity, the garden has been transformed from a very sterile-looking suburban yard to a diverse woodland planting with little paths winding through rolling terrain; large, beautiful shade trees; and dozens of species of choice perennials. Paradise in a little over a decade!

The owner did not perform all these miracles at once, however. She removed sod, planted trees, and planted wildflowers, then mulched with wood chips acquired from a tree service. Her winding paths are graveled with small, irregular, natural-looking gravel, which was screened out of her planting beds and carried to the paths one bucket at a time. As her trees grow and cast more shade, she removes sun-loving perennials and replaces them with woodland plants.

A diverse garden encourages more diversity. If you keep your mind, heart, and senses open, your garden will enrich and inspire you with wonderful displays of wildlife as well as interesting new color combinations that you would never have thought of yourself (and you may or may not like).

A Short Digression on Color

For those of us who are blessed with color vision, color is a riveting phenomenon. Color is used by insects, fish, birds, mammals, and flowers to signal: Danger! Food! Warning! and Hey there, come up and see me sometime! Human color preferences are extremely personal because colors can affect different people in many different ways.

I once jumped out of our not-quite-stopped van when we drove up to a job and discovered that the unlabeled azalea that we had transplanted several months before had burst into hot pink bloom right in front of a genista which was in full, screaming-yellow bloom. The combination was too eye-popping for comfort, and the azalea needed to be transplanted immediately.

Though pure bright colors harmonize, mixed colors, like mixed drinks, can be nauseating. All the spectral colors of the rainbow (violet, indigo, blue, green, yellow, orange, and red) get along with each other, and all the primary pigment colors (red, yellow, and blue) work together as well.

Unfortunately, some colors, most notably reds, clash with themselves: It is very hard to find a pure red with no blue or orange overtones. Red usually tends toward crimson, which is a bluish red, or toward scarlet, which is an orangish red. Bluish red and orangish red clash violently.

Though pure yellow harmonizes well with many colors, greenish yellow and orangish yellow make a nauseating pair.

Blue is the most easygoing color; greenish blues and violet blues harmonize well together as well as with most other colors. The secondary colors—orange, green and purple—can be startlingly bright next to each other, and produce interesting optical illusions, but aside from those compounded of feuding reds, they don't actually clash.

There are a lot of compound colors with fancy names, which I only know about because I looked them up. These are often "muddy" colors, which are more difficult to use than the clearer, purer colors.

For example, mauve and puce are both complications of purple. Puce's namesake was a blood-filled flea. If you want to see mauve, look in the mirror and stick out your tongue.

Chartreuse is a screamingly bright, light yellowish green. Ochre is a brownish, orangish yellow. Salmon is a pinkish orange, coral is an orangish pink. They are all temperamental colors that clash with almost everything.

Foliage doesn't display the dizzying variety of colors that flowers do, but a clashing tree can be much more disturbing than a couple of dueling petunias. Colors that are acceptable in flowers can sometimes be overwhelming when encountered in foliage.

Unfortunately, due to the existence of variegated foliage, it is possible for plants to clash with themselves. I don't want to name any names, but there are some shrubs out there with variegated yellow green and yellowish orange leaves, and bluish pink flowers. This is the vegetative equivalent of wearing a gold plaid jacket, green plaid pants, and a shirt with red and white polka dots.

In the fall the dress code loosens up: anything goes.

Garden Colors for the Color-blind

My grandfather was color-blind. He couldn't tell the difference in color between an orange and a piece of toast. If you are color-blind, or even just color-deaf, you can plant for fragrance, taste, texture and form, sun and shade, and have just as much fun as the color junkies. Here are a few simple color rules you can follow, so you can avoid committing any color faux pas.

1. Colored leaves are wonderful in the autumn, avoid them at all other times of the year.

2. Avoid variegated leaves.

3. White, lemon yellow, blue, or violet flowers will never clash with each other. Avoid all others unless you have a color-wise friend to help you choose.

The Inquiring Gardener

Perhaps the last bastion of true American individuality, mostly un-connected to commercialism, is the American garden. The garden is a wonderful place to experiment, as long as you keep the precept "do no harm" in mind. Use your garden as a laboratory in which to set up experiments to produce joy. If a particular plant fails to please, move on; give perennials to someone who will enjoy them, and don't replant annuals that disappointed you. Remember, young plants are easily moved. Nothing is permanent except death, and if nothing ever died, what would we have to put in our compost piles?

An informal garden which is allowed to evolve as it grows can completely transcend the gardener's original intentions. Serendip-ity is a wonderful designer: a felled evergreen may lie in a perfect spot to plant a wildlife hedge, or an upended bucket may suggest a good spot for a big rock. Seedlings can germinate in amazing loca-tions. Until it was remodeled a couple of years ago, one of our downtown buildings had a six-foot-tall birch sapling growing out of a cornice.

For many years we had a landscaping job that included planting about two dozen window boxes outside the first and second floors of the buildings. My favorite window box was in deep shade and had small ferns growing upside down out of the bottom of the box.

Chapter Five

The Care and Feeding of an ORGANIC GARDEN

arden maintenance *is what separates the* gardeners from the landscapers.

Gardens really are like children: when they're new, they're little and cute and the plants stay where they're planted; later, they can get a bit gangly and unruly, and tend to reach beyond their allotted places. In maturity, children and gardens can surprise their caretakers with unexpected conjunctions and combinations that can be extremely interesting, and often useful.

Sometimes there is no such thing as a second chance with people, or with life choices. A dead relative cannot be resurrected; cutting words cannot be unspoken. But in a garden, there is always next year. Most "mistakes" can be fixed; perennials, shrubs, and young trees can be moved. Annoying annuals need never be used again, unruly squash plants can be planted farther from the better-behaved vegetables, new trees can be planted to take the place of those that have kicked the flowerpot. Of course, really old trees are not truly replaceable in one human lifetime, but planting an heir is the right thing to do.

Like fine people and fine wines, gardens improve with age; it is only after the saplings have matured to trees, the brick has begun to weather, the rocks to grow moss, and the bronze has acquired a patina that a garden becomes a presence. Even the most symmetrical, clumsy, and over-obvious landscape designs will become more beautiful as the plants mature, especially if the gardener tweaks things around and plays with the garden over the years. Only healthy plants however are capable of reaching old age; the unhealthy tend to die young, spindly, and unattractive.

It takes an entire healthy ecosystem to produce healthy plants. As I mentioned earlier, laying down a layer of well-aged herbivore manure or compost is the quickest and easiest way to build up the soil before planting a new garden; it is also the easiest way to maintain the soil in top condition to grow most plants.

There are, of course, exceptions to every rule. Plants can vary widely in their nutritional needs. Some benefit from huge feedings, while others get indigestion from any feeding at all. It is a good idea to look up the nutritional requirements of your plants before giving them compost. Any plant that is described as liking sandy soil, poor soil, or dry soil is unlikely to perform well if it is planted in rich, moist, humusy soil. Rich moist soil can be fatal to cacti for instance.

Rising to the Challenge

Adversity strengthens the character of many herbs: marjoram, oregano, lavender, thyme, and rosemary are all drought-tolerant Mediterranean natives that lose much of their character and become rather bland if they are coddled. Like other drought-tolerant plants, they are partial to alkaline soils—if your soil tends to be acidic and slow-draining, a thin layer of limestone or marble landscaping gravel on the bottom of the planting hole will help improve the drainage and add a bit of needed alkalinity. Mixing a handful of powdered limestone or crushed eggshells in with the planting soil will also help. If you top the whole thing off with a limestone or marble gravel mulch, your herbs will feel right at home.

For Acid-Loving Plants

Garden compost or composted manure may be too alkaline for acid-loving plants such as rhododendrons, azaleas, blueberries, citrus, and camellias. Buy a package of peat moss at a nursery or garden center before planting acid-loving plants. Mix some peat moss in with the soil when planting these acid-lovers, then keep them well mulched with pine needles, which are also acidic. Treat your acid-loving plants to a refreshing beverage by watering them with your old coffee and tea; coffee grounds and tea leaves also make a lovely acidic mulch.

Seedling Husbandry

Though many vegetables and showy flowers need very rich soil, their seeds, like all other seeds, contain their own food supply, and tend to rot if they germinate in rich soil. In order to reduce seed mortality, commercial seed starting mixes are sterilized and formulated to be very low in soil nutrients.

I had trouble with vegetable growing for years until I realized that the soil in my vegetable garden was too rich for seeds. Now I let my seeds germinate in soil left "as is" after the previous season's crops, and wait until the seedlings grow their first real leaves before feeding them compost.

Mulch, Breakfast of Champions

While composted materials become one with the soil immediately, several inches of uncomposted material (a.k.a. mulch) lying on the surface of the soil helps moderate soil temperatures, smothers weed seeds, and conserves surface moisture. Seeds germinate best in unmulched soil, but once the plants are up, a mulched garden requires far less maintenance than does an unmulched garden.

Mulch can be almost any nontoxic material that allows air and water to reach the soil. I have seen all the following organic materials used to conserve soil moisture and discourage weeds: leaves, cocoa hulls, pine needles, rice hulls, grape pomace, compost, shredded wood and bark, old wool blankets, and rugs. Abundant mulching materials will vary from place to place. Needless to say, some mulches are prettier than others, and materials which may be fine for a utilitarian vegetable garden may not be attractive enough for an ornamental garden. The prettiest organic mulches tend to be dark-colored and fine-grained.

While the most common mulches are organic and add humus to the soil as they break down, plants that are adapted to arid climates, and thrive in poor, dry soil, may suffer if bedded down with an organic mulch. Stones may be the most suitable mulch for a very dry climate. I am referring here to stones laid on the arid ground, not to the ubiquitous gravel-over-plastic, which smothers and decimates soil life.

A well-mulched bed is a thing of beauty and a joy (not forever, because organic mulch eventually decomposes and must be replaced). Some mulches are an olfactory pleasure: the mingled scents of hot pine needles and hot strawberries on a summer's day are one of life's exquisite pleasures.

Because mulch does tend to hold moisture, it should be kept away from tree trunks and woody plant stems, to prevent the bark from rotting.

Water Is Life

In general, the less watering you have to do, the healthier your plants will be. Plants adapt to dry conditions by slowing their growth rate, and growing more root hairs to seek out water; watering upsets these adaptations. Frequent and shallow watering encourages roots to grow near the soil's surface rather than to dive deep where they can reach subsoil water, so one skipped watering may kill the plant. Mulched gardens often don't need to be watered at all, since the soil retains its moisture better under mulch. Humusy, well-mulched soil acts as a reservoir of water for the plants growing in it. For the sake of our plants' health, we should let the soil do its job as much as possible. If you must water your plants, water them infrequently and deeply, otherwise you may kill them with kindness.

Used Water

Water is one of the most precious substances on earth. As the world's population increases, watering plants with potable water will become less and less acceptable. Recycling water at home will no doubt be the wave of the future. Here are a few flavors of secondhand water that plants really enjoy:

•Acid-loving plants such as blueberries, azaleas, rhododendrons, heathers, and citruses all enjoy a little drink of cold coffee or tea now and then.

• The water used to boil eggs is odorless and perfectly fine for indoor use.

• The water used to rinse out milk bottles or cartons can be used to water outdoor plants. Tomatoes, eggplants, petunias, peppers, and potatoes all benefit from milky water because milk kills tobacco mosaic virus, which can afflict these related plants. Milky water also helps protect cabbages from cabbage worms.

(continued)

> • *Rather than pouring the cooking water from vegetables down the drain, use it for watering. Your plants will benefit from the vitamins and minerals in the water. Better yet, use the vegetable water in soups and reap the benefits yourself. Some vegetable water is unsuitable for indoor use: beet water should not be used on houseplants unless you have a dark pink rug, and broccoli water becomes quite smelly as it ages.*

Seeds need to be kept moist in order to germinate, and young seedlings need to be kept moist until their roots are several inches long. When the weather doesn't cooperate, watering becomes a necessity. We have rain barrels beneath all of our downspouts, and except during prolonged drought, they are more than sufficient for all our watering needs.

Hesitate Before Weeding

After a long winter, it is all too easy to mistake your prized perennials or seedling flowers for weeds. Labeling your perennials in the summer will help, as will acquiring some well-illustrated garden plant and weed identification books. Your garden will fill in much more quickly if you refrain from reflexively pulling all new seedlings before identifying them.

Prune Out the Superfluous

Though a good pruning book is as essential a pruning tool as a saw or lopper, and the necessary detail of a pruning book is well beyond the scope of this book, there are a few basic pruning techniques that are so important to plant health that I am including them here.

Plant bark acts as a barrier to keep out bacteria and fungi (we call our own bark "skin"). Any break in this barrier makes a plant more susceptible to infection. When a tree or woody shrub is wounded, bark grows sideways from the edges of the wound to heal it. Bark can grow across a one-inch wound in one growing season, but it cannot grow around a corner. This is why branch stubs tend to die back to the trunk. Rot can then spread from the stubs to the main trunk. Trees and woody shrubs—lilacs and camellias for instance—should never be given "haircuts" unless you are trying to kill them. Shearing is for hedges; trees and shrubs must be pruned, carefully.

The least traumatic way to prune plants is to pinch off unwanted growth while it is still very small and soft. If you don't procrastinate, the only tools you will need are your fingers. Pinch off the tender young growth using your fingernails, or gently rub buds off with your fingers. This preemptive pruning leaves an almost negligible wound. The phrase "nipping it in the bud" refers to this practice of stopping potential problems while they are still small and easy to deal with.

If you failed to nip unwanted growth in the bud, you will need to use tools. Pruning tools should be as sharp as possible: dull pruners don't cut cleanly. Wipe pruning blades with alcohol to disinfect them before moving from one plant to another, to avoid spreading disease. Cleaning the blades between cuts even on the same plant is also not a bad idea.

A branch should be pruned back either to another branch or to

the tree's trunk. It is possible to prune too close to the trunk, again making it difficult for the tree to heal the wound. A slightly bulging "collar" marks the spot where the branch emerges from the trunk. Branches should be pruned back just to where they meet the collar, thus leaving a smaller

wound and more intact bark to grow across the wound. Painting a little aloe vera juice or gel over the open wound will help it heal more quickly, and the bitter aloe taste repels insects.

If you have to saw off a large branch, first make an undercut by sawing upward from the underside of the branch about a foot from the trunk, then saw all the way down through the branch farther out from the trunk. The weight of a heavy branch usually breaks it before it is sawn all the way through. If you haven't made an undercut, the falling branch can tear the bark and damage the trunk. But if there is an undercut, the bark will only rip back as far as the undercut, sparing the trunk from damage. Once most of the weight of the branch is removed, the stub can be pruned back to the bark collar.

"Getting rid of the dead wood" is an expression with an agricultural origin: a tree with dead limbs is not only a potential danger to passers-under, it is itself in danger of disease. Dead limbs should be pruned off trees and shrubs.

The Self-perpetuating Garden

Though there is no such thing as a no-maintenance garden, there is an enormous difference between high-maintenance and low-maintenance gardens. I am biased toward well-adjusted gardens that don't require coddling merely to survive. I have long dreamt of a self-propagating vegetable garden, and have eagerly watched for self-seeding vegetables. For years I have had a very reliable red-leafed mustard that I transplant into place every spring.

A few summers ago I thought I was well on my way to a reliably self-sowing lettuce until I walked into our kitchen after an evening class and found my husband busily cooking dinner. A perfectly lovely salad was already on the table. As I looked at the salad, I suddenly recognized it as my prize lettuce, the most beautiful, huge, perfect head of lettuce I had ever grown, a Red Sails butter crunch with an eighteen-inch diameter. I began laughing and crying and exclaiming "You killed my pet lettuce!"

My husband looked extremely sheepish. I had informed him that very morning that since that gor-geous lettuce had seeded itself from a plant I'd grown the previous year, I was-n't going to harm a leaf of its head that year. I was going to let it be my stud let-tuce, to father (and mother) my longed-for herd of cold-hardy naturalized lettuce.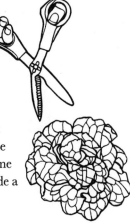

When he'd gone out to pick greens, my better half had been overcome by the radiant beauty of my pet lettuce, and had cut the whole plant, instead of just pulling off some leaves. The second he cut it, he knew he'd made a mistake.

Though I tried to baby the poor mutilated stub along, hoping that it would somehow survive to produce seed, it rotted, then died. My poor husband attained some notoriety among our friends for his wanton lettuce murder.

Chapter Six

Pests: Learning from YOUR ENEMIES

I will always treasure my memory of watching a squirrel traveling upside down, hand over hand, across twenty feet of cable strung between two trees to get to the bird feeder in the middle of the span. Merely watching birds on the feeder could never have given me the pleasure that acrobatic squirrel did.

There are many possible ways of squirrel-proofing a bird feeder, but eventually squirrels can outwit most humans in order to get to birdseed. Anyone who has ever driven in a squirrel-infested area knows that squirrels are not geniuses. But you don't have to be a genius to solve most problems, all you need is persistence. If you try to solve a problem from every possible angle, eventually you will probably succeed. This is what squirrels do when trying to crack the code of a squirrel-proof feeder.

When you look at things from the squirrels' point of view, it becomes much more obvious why they are so persistent: they are trying to keep their babies fed with "our" birdseed, and they are trying to keep their babies sheltered under our roofs. Their motivation for getting into our stuff is much stronger than ours is for keeping them out. Every waking hour, except during the mating season, squirrels are thinking about how to get into that bird feeder, or how to get into that attic, and then testing their hypotheses. I hope no human is that single-minded about protecting birdseed!

There have been agricultural pests as long as there has been agriculture, and for as long as there have been pests, humans have been trying to control them. Some of these controls have been based on experience and observation, others have been less scientific.

In ancient times, religion, ritual, and magic were important pest-control methods. The methods didn't necessarily work, but they made people feel better. In classical Rome, placating the gods was considered good for general-purpose plant protection; so was touching a plant with a red dogwood twig; and placing a mare's skull on a stake in the middle of a garden was supposed to protect the garden from evil influences. (As I mentioned in my previous book, *Slug Bread & Beheaded Thistles,* fresh deer skulls are not an effective deer repellent.) I doubt that a mare's skull would be any more useful in protecting a garden unless horses are more sensitive about their deceased friends than deer are, and the garden is being attacked by horses.

Modern pest-control methods can also be based on ritual and magic rather than on scientific information. The average homeowner who sprays a pesticide without reading the label first is performing an action that is no more scientific than putting a horse skull on a stake.

Creating Pests

I have on occasion seen people upset, seemingly out of all proportion, by "pests" in their gardens. Flying into a fury because chinch bugs made a brown spot in the lawn, or because a mole tunneled under it, strikes me as a bit of an overreaction.

We are, after all, responsible for transforming these organisms into pests. Most animals do not become pests unless humans unbalance the environment, leaving the critters with either a surplus of food, a paucity of predators, a lack of competition, or all of the above. This principle works the same for organisms ranging from the very large, like deer, whose natural predators were hunted down like vermin for a couple of centuries, on down to tiny grass-sucking chinch bugs, which have flourished in the huge expanses of cornfields and on the vast green deserts of America's lawns.

Out of Control...

Sometimes our efforts to "control" pests go so wildly awry that it would be comical if it weren't so sad.

Two years after the start of a public health campaign to eradicate malaria in Malaysia, village roofs began to collapse. The palm thatch roofs had been sprayed with DDT to kill the mosquitoes that transmit malaria, and the spraying had killed off the parasitic wasps that normally preyed on the caterpillars that ate the thatch. After their roofs started to collapse, the Malaysians were attacked by bedbugs which previously had been kept in check by ants that fed on the bedbug larvae. The ants had been eradicated by the DDT, but the bedbugs were resistant.

When DDT was used to control the codling moth in North America and Great Britain, it not only made red spider mites breed faster, it also killed off their natural predators. All this encouragement changed the red spider mite from a relatively harmless arachnid into a major pest of fruit trees.

Mercifully, the sale and use of DDT has been banned in the United States since 1973. Unfortunately, we now have other chemicals that may be just as bad, and we have them in greater numbers than ever before.

Knowledge Is Power

A lot of pesticide use could be avoided if the people who are responsible for selling plant materials and pesticides made sure their customers were well informed about the true nature of their purchases.

Pesticides Cannot Prevent Old Age

I once talked a neighbor in California out of spraying his snapdragons with Diazinon to save them from the insects that were "killing them." It was autumn, and the snapdragons, being annuals, were dying of old age; weak plants attract insects as inevitably as an old wildebeest attracts lions. Our neighbor had bought his snapdragons at a nursery, and had not been informed that snapdragons are annuals. After I explained that his snapdragons were dying of old age, and there was nothing he could do to save them, he immediately stopped spraying.

Herbicides Are Useless Against Concrete

Mrs. Fastidious, of the manicured landscape, routinely pulled every single weed out of every single crack in her sidewalk and driveway, then poured a contact herbicide in the cracks. She discontinued this practice when we informed her that contact herbicides only work when they are applied to foliage. Pouring them on concrete does nothing to prevent future weed growth.

White Flies Love Malathion

When we first visited Mrs. Fastidious's garden, white flies covered most of her plants, and she sprayed malathion on them once a week. I had never seen a white fly in my life before I encountered them in her backyard. Her yard, she informed us through clenched teeth, drove her crazy. The yard looked simple, but it was very high maintenance: the garden equivalent of a white suit.

We took one look at her white flies, glanced inside her garden shed, which seemed to contain enough house and garden poisons to finish off every living thing in the county, and gently suggested she try using insecticidal soap. She was willing to try, so we brought her a bottle of Safer's Soap. She loved it, and happily sprayed with it every week. (Insecticidal soap is specially formulated not to foam up so it doesn't clog spray bottles. It is sold in nurseries and garden centers.)

Unlike chemical pesticides, soap sprays are generally harmless to beneficial insects. Since the soap spray didn't kill off the white flies' predators, the white flies eventually disappeared.

Please Read the Labels

In the immortal words on all pesticide labels: "It is a violation of federal law to use this product in a manner inconsistent with its labeling." I truly believe that it is darn near impossible to use chemical pesticides in the manner prescribed on the labels. I have seen many, many instances of professional chemical applicators misusing pesticides: not wearing protective clothing, spraying on windy days, spraying in the rain, spraying near a waterway…. The professionals do this because they have to make a living in this world and cannot wait for the perfect windless day in a guaranteed string of rainless days.

People often assume that because chemical pesticides and herbicides are sold over the counter, that they are somehow harmless. This can be a very dangerous assumption. A former next-door neighbor of ours was housebound for many years due to severe, permanent lung damage caused by pesticide misuse: she had been working late when a maintenance man, thinking that the building was empty, used a pesticide to kill barn swallows nesting under the eaves. The fumes ruined her lungs.

The pesticide he used was definitely not registered for killing birds.

Accident Prevention for the Absentminded

I have an extremely poor short-term memory, so very early in life I had to learn not to set up my own accidents. On the very rare occasions when my accident-prevention habits lapse, the predictable always happens. The only time I left a hammer on top of a ladder, I moved the ladder and the hammer landed on my head. The only time I ever put something on the roof of my car, I drove off and lost our son's bicycle helmet.

I don't want to give the impression that I am averse to risk-taking. I am not, but I carefully decide which risks I am willing to take and which risks I am not. I am willing to risk ridicule, disdain, hostility, gaudy color combinations, exhaustion, failed experiments, public failure, spilled milk . . . all of which I have experienced, repeatedly. But I am not willing to risk causing permanent harm to humans, the environment, or wildlife. I am completely unwilling to use garden chemicals: I consider the risk unacceptable.

If I do a bad job of fertilizing with compost, at worst I may end up with beanless bean plants, or flowerless nasturtiums; if I use rhubarb leaf tea as a pesticide and make a mistake, I might kill a few caterpillars that were planning to be butterflies rather than moths, but I will never end up poisoning an entire building or polluting a stream.

Murphy's Law

When Captain Edward Murphy Jr., an engineer at Edwards Air Force Base, formulated his famous law— "If there's more than one way to do a job and one of those ways will end in disaster, then somebody will do it that way" —he was reacting to a series of plane crashes which had been caused by the improper installation of gravity gauges. Murphy was an avid proponent of designed-in foolproofing and urged the development of gravity gauges that would only fit into the control panel one way: the right way.

Guinea Pigs
Human, Adult

In 1998, the scientific advisory panel of the Environmental Protection Agency (EPA), which consisted of doctors, ethicists, and scientists, concluded that human testing of pesticides "to facilitate the interests of industry or of agriculture" is unjustifiable. The EPA formally instituted a moratorium on using the results of such tests.

In November of 2001, however, after a change of administration, the EPA announced that it would use safety data from pesticide testing conducted on human subjects to set pesticide safety standards. There was such an uproar that in December 2001 the EPA reversed itself, temporarily reinstated the moratorium on human testing, and asked the National Academy of Sciences to recommend whether such research is ethical or scientifically useful.

Currently, researchers conducting animal experiments try to find the maximum dose of any given chemical that produces no adverse effects. Because humans and animals are different, the EPA then adds a safety factor of ten, making the maximum allowable legal limit for human exposure one tenth of the "no effect" level determined by animal testing. If a chemical is tested on humans, that extra safety factor is eliminated. It is possible that the prospect of selling ten times more product has piqued the industry's interest in human testing.

Chemical manufacturers are extremely eager to conduct human testing. Some of the tests they submitted to the EPA in 2001 for evaluation involved paying "volunteers" to swallow doses of pesticides hundreds of times greater than levels previously considered safe by the EPA. Though many of the "volunteers" developed headaches, nausea, and vomiting after drinking the poison, company scientists concluded that the symptoms were unrelated to the chemicals.

Human, Infant

A growing number of studies demonstrate that prenatal exposure to endocrine-disrupting chemicals such as PCBs (polychlorinated biphenyl), phthalates, and dioxins affects brain development and intelligence. These man-made chlorinated compounds are commonly found in pesticides, herbicides, and fungicides. Dioxins are also commonly produced when plastics are burned: NEVER burn plastics!

In the 1970s, Dr. Joseph Jacobson of Wayne State University began studying the prenatal effects of PCBs. Fisherman who ate large amounts of fish from Lake Michigan had been found to have very high blood concentrations of PCBs, and Dr. Jacobson wondered what effect the PCBs would have on babies born to mothers who ate large amounts of Lake Michigan fish.

The infants' PCB exposure was estimated by testing blood from the umbilical cord, the mother's PCB blood levels, and the mother's milk. The infants with the highest prenatal PCB exposures exhibited poorer short-term memories, shorter attention spans, cognitive problems, and were three times more likely to score in the bottom fifteenth percentile of IQ tests. Postnatal exposure did not cause such significant problems.

If a frog is put in a pot of hot water, it will immediately jump out. But if a frog is put in a pot of cold water and the water is heated up very slowly, the hapless animal will not notice the gradual increase in temperature and will eventually boil to death without  ever trying to jump out of the pot. If chemicals erode our species' intelligence very, very gradually and imperceptibly, we may not notice that there is a problem before we become too stupid to jump out of the pot.

Amphibians

In 1995, Minnesota schoolchildren first discovered deformed frogs with either missing limbs or one or two extras. By 2000, deformed amphibians had been found in forty-four states, affecting thirty-eight species of frogs and nineteen species of toads. Deformed frogs have also been discovered in Canada and Japan.

Under "normal" circumstances, 2 percent or less of an amphibian population might be expected to have malformations, yet surveys of some ponds in agricultural areas found that 60 percent of the frogs were malformed.

The cause of the deformities has yet to be determined, but most scientists believe that a combination of environmental factors is responsible. The main suspects are increased ultraviolet radiation due to atmospheric ozone depletion, parasites, and chemical pollutants, especially the "endocrine disrupters" that mimic the action of natural hormones.

A U.S. Geological Survey report dated March 29, 2000, stated: "the situation requires urgent attention. These die-offs and deformities of amphibians around the globe are of great concern because amphibians are good barometers of significant environmental changes that may go initially undetected by humans."

Boy Frog Meets Boy/ Girl Frog Meets Boy/ Boy/Boy Frog

As I was getting ready to send this book's manuscript to the publisher, some very interesting research about frogs was published in the April 16, 2002, issue of the Proceedings of the National Academy of Sciences: *developmental endocrinologist Dr. Tyrone B. Hayes and colleagues reported that exposure to very low concentrations of atrazine, which is the most commonly used herbicide in North America, turns male tadpoles into hermaphrodites. The EPA's maximum allowable limit for atrazine concentrations in drinking water is 3 parts per billion (ppb), a concentration which is 30 times higher than the 0.1 ppb which caused hermaphroditism in tadpoles. Some of the unfortunate amphibians had both ovaries and testes, others had multiple sex organs (one over-endowed frog had six testes). Adult male frogs that were exposed to atrazine as tadpoles had testosterone levels that were lower than the levels seen in normal females. These reproductive mutations can only be seen through a microscope, and had not been discovered by previous researchers who were investigating the effects of higher doses of atrazine.*

After successfully repeating their experiment fifty-one times, Dr. Hayes and his colleagues went on a field trip to the Midwest, where they found many native leopard frogs (Rana pipiens) *that had reproductive anomalies similar to the defects induced by atrazine in the laboratory. Atrazine levels of up to 40 ppb have been measured in rainwater in the Midwest, and levels of up to several parts per million have been measured in agricultural runoff.*

Dr. Hayes stated that since atrazine has been widely used for forty years, it is possible that it may be one of the factors responsible for the global decline of amphibians.

Playing God Is Not a Good Idea

No matter how dangerous, annoying, or economically detrimental a "pest" appears to be, we are not wise enough to safely conclude that we would be better off without it. Some fierce and dangerous pests inhabit extremely delicate and environmentally valuable areas. Eradicating them might do the world immeasurable harm.

Throughout most of human history, the danger of malaria has prevented humans from settling near swamps. The draining and "reclamation" of wetlands is a relatively recent phenomenon. After draining a large percentage of our wetlands, we have finally learned why wetlands should not be drained. It appears that they function as Mother Earth's kidneys, absorbing water and filtering out impurities before the water continues its journey to the sea.

Cumulative Effects

for want of a nail, the shoe was lost;
for want of the shoe, the horse was lost;
for want of the horse, the rider was lost;
for want of the rider, the battle was lost;
for want of the battle, the kingdom was lost;
And all from the want of a horseshoe nail.

Since time before memory, people in India have believed in powerful earth demons that guard the Earth and all her waters. Anyone approaching a body of water might be accosted by its guardian *yaksha,* and asked a riddle. Those who answered incorrectly were ritually sacrificed by the demon.

The Mahabharata, India's national epic, contains an account of its five heroic brothers, the Pandavas, encountering the demon of a lake. The four younger brothers, driven by thirst, ignored the demon's riddle and were killed. Only the eldest, Yudhishthira, answered the riddle.

The demon asked: "What is the greatest wonder in life?"

Yudhishthira answered: "That every man must one day die, yet every man lives as if he were immortal."

The demon approved of the answer, and rewarded Yudhishthira by bringing his brothers back to life.

The ancient mythmakers obviously realized that the wrong attitude toward water brought death.

Diversity Is Another Word for Richness

In 1915, the Mexican boll weevil, which had already devastated cotton crops in much of the South, reached Coffee County, Alabama. Coffee County was largely a one-crop county, its finances almost completely dependent on the production of cotton.

The boll weevil, as expected, devastated the cotton crop and the economy. But one far-thinking businessman who lived in Enterprise, Coffee County's biggest city, took matters into his own hands. He bribed a heavily indebted cotton farmer to try peanut farming for a year.

The peanut crop was such a success that the farmer was able to pay off his debts and put money in the bank. Seeing this, many of Coffee County's farmers diversified their crops, growing peanuts, hay, sugar cane, corn, and potatoes; some even began dairies. Prosperity followed diversity, as it usually does.

A monument to the boll weevil was dedicated on December 11, 1919. The inscription on the statue reads: "In profound appreciation to the Boll Weevil and what it has done as the herald of prosperity."

A far more famous animal monument is the seagull monument in Salt Lake City, which commemorates the Salt Lake seagulls that, in the spring of 1848, descended upon and devoured the plagues of locusts that were destroying the sprouting crops of the Mormon pioneers.

Many witnesses attributed the birds' timely arrival to divine intervention. The seagull monument was unveiled in Temple Square on September 13, 1913.

The Achilles' Heel Approach to Pest Control

My favorite way to control pests is to use their predilections and weaknesses against them. This style of pest control is very similar to playing poker—she who understands her opponents best, wins:

Warm-Blooded Pests

THE BETTER MOUSETRAP... is a heavy-duty five-gallon bucket! The mouse's curiosity is the bait. A little peanut butter or grain doesn't hurt either. Over the years we have found dead mice in buckets of bird seed and assumed they died of thirst, in buckets during the dead of winter and assumed they died of exposure, and in buckets with a little bit of water in them and assumed they drowned. It finally dawned on me after I found a dead deer mouse in an empty bucket in my greenhouse that the bait was the bucket itself—and curiosity had killed the mouse.

To set a bucket trap, either place the bucket next to an object that the mouse will have no trouble climbing, or make a mouse-size rope ladder from the ground to the top of the bucket by tying a long piece of twine to the bucket handle. Once the mouse has fallen into the bucket, it won't be able to jump out. If your area has a severe mouse shortage, and you don't want to further deplete the population, you can carry the mouse, bucket and all, to another location to be set free. If you don't set it free, the mouse will expire rather rapidly.

Many species of voles, which are cute, pudgy, mouselike little creatures, eat roots and tubers. Try baiting a two- or three-gallon bucket with a nice juicy carrot if you are having vole trouble; voles have short little legs, and a five-gallon bucket may be too tall for them to climb into.

Caution: If young children wander on your property, *please* put buckets and other large containers out of their reach! A small child who falls headfirst into a bucket can easily suffocate because a small fat bottom can form an airtight seal. We know a young man who, many years ago, almost lost his life while head down in a large ceramic vase.

DEERLY UNBELOVED Deer have extremely thin legs that are fairly easily broken. Although they can jump fences that are up to nine feet high, loose wire fencing billowing on the ground can stymie them. Deer cannot afford to get their skinny little legs caught in wire, so they will not walk over or stand in wire fencing.

Place the fencing where the deer will need to stand in order to eat the plant you are trying to protect. Our friend Jim tasted apples from his most isolated apple tree for the first time the year he ringed his trees with wire fencing.

THE INVISIBLE EGRESS Deer and rabbits tend to avoid entering areas without visible escape routes. My friend Susie's vegetable garden has a row of pines on one side and a fence on the other. Though the deer are perfectly free to walk through the pines and into the garden, they never do. The solid visual barrier of the pines and the actual barrier of the fence must give Susie's garden the appearance of a dangerous deer trap.

Though animals will tend to avoid entering areas that are obviously closed in, the semi-invisible barriers created by wire fencing can confuse them. One late-winter day I returned from running errands and was dismayed to discover a rampaging cottontail rabbit inside my fenced-in vegetable plot. It had squeezed under the gate and apparently had forgotten where the hole was. It was frantically jumping at the fence, and violently bouncing off again. I opened the gate and herded the rabbit out. I doubt I will ever see that particular rabbit anywhere near my vegetable garden again.

SMOOTH SKIN AND NO RABBITS Aloe vera juice, which is so soothing to sunburned, abraded, or cut skin, as well as to newly pruned branches, is very bitter, and will prevent rabbits from nibbling on plants.

THE SHIRT OFF YOUR BACK A stinky, sweat-soaked shirt will repel raccoons for a couple of days, or until it gets rained on. Our neighbor John also informs me that a stinky undershirt stopped beavers from finishing a dam they were building on his property, but after a month the scent must have worn off, because the beavers finished the dam and built his shirt right into it.

PRESERVE YOUR FRUIT WITH SUGAR Researchers at Cornell University discovered that spraying ripening berries with sugar water helped protect the fruit from birds. Fruit-loving birds can only digest simple sugars like fructose; more complex sugars, like sucrose, upset their stomachs.

The Official Cornell Sugar Water Recipe: dissolve eleven pounds of sugar (yes, that's eleven pounds!) in one gallon of warm water. Let it sit until the sugar is completely dissolved and the solution looks clear. Then spray the sugar solution onto ripening blueberries, strawberries, or other fruit.

I tested this recipe in my kitchen, and amazingly, eleven pounds of sugar does dissolve completely in a gallon of water.

IT'S A BIRD! IT'S A PLANE! Birds seem to be affected by grape flavoring in the same way mammals are affected by hot peppers. There is a commercial goose repellent that contains the artificial grape flavoring that gives grape drinks and bubblegum their flavor. The repellent is registered as a feeding repellent for geese and other birds, and is one of the repellents recommended by the FAA to help keep birds away from airport airspaces. It is sprayed on airport lawns to prevent geese from grazing.

HOT AND SPICY Hot peppers, as many of us have learned the hard way, can cause great discomfort to mammals, as well as to many other organisms ranging from caterpillars to zebra mussels. Last summer I used powdered cayenne pepper to chase away a red squirrel that was menacing a phoebes' nest above our back door. I had heard the parent phoebes squawking about something, and went outside to investigate. One parent was on the nest; the other was flying around frantically trying to drive off the red squirrel that was pacing on the railing below the nest.

Red squirrels are notorious nest-robbers, so I went inside and got some cayenne, and sprinkled it so liberally on the railing and stair landing that my eyes started to burn. (Interestingly, birds seem completely immune to pepper-induced pain.) I went back in the house, and in an hour or so I heard a squirrel making an enormous racket.

Much to my delight, the phoebes successfully raised two nest loads of chicks; we need all the insect-eaters we can get!

Cold-Blooded Pests

SPICED INSECTS Entomologist Dr. Geoff Zehnder tested the effectiveness of using hot peppers to protect plants from insect pests. Two years of testing in the cabbage patch proved that hot pepper was a more effective caterpillar repellent than the chemical insecticide lambda-cyhalothrin.

Dr. Zehnder's recipe: two tablespoons McCormick Hot Red Pepper, and six drops of liquid dish soap dissolved in a gallon of water. Stir the solution and spray your plants with it weekly.

If you are partial to another hot pepper brand, I'm sure it would work as well.

BEETLE MANIA I am a worm wrangler; I grow composting worms and set up vermicomposting systems for people. My worm bins are quite large, and rounding up worms can be very time consuming, so a few years ago I began trying to lure them into plastic cups for easier pickings.

I had already discovered that worms love to congregate in half coconut shells with the meat still in them, but since coconuts aren't grown locally and tend to be a bit expensive, I attempted to find an alternative. I tried small cups of solid shortening, peanut butter, and oil, and eventually realized that large numbers of bark beetles were drowning in the oil. (I had been having trouble with bark beetles which had been introduced into my bins with some wood chips. Big mistake, but that's how I learn.) I immediately switched my emphasis from attracting and holding worms to trapping and killing beetles.

The oiled beetles quickly began to stink, so I began testing the beetle-attracting effects of various other liquids. When I tried white vinegar, Eureka! Bark beetles began drowning by the thousands. Zombielike armies of bark beetles marched toward the cups of vinegar like lemmings toward a cliff. I had to empty a quarter inch of pickled beetles out of the cups every week until, after a month or so, the beetle population crashed. Now I am anxious to test vinegar as a trap for other beetle species.

BEETLE ADDICTS Japanese beetles cannot resist eating *Geranium maculatum* (a wild perennial geranium with tiny pink flowers), though it invariably proves to be their last meal. Other geraniums are also attractive to Japanese beetles, but they only knock the beetles out for eight hours at a time, not permanently. If you have Japanese beetle trouble, these pretty little wildflowers should look doubly attractive.

GLUTTONY WILL GET YOU NOWHERE If your petunias, and their cousins the tomatoes, potatoes, and eggplants, are being eaten by Colorado potato beetles, try dusting their leaves early in the morning with dry wheat bran or cornmeal. The beetles will ingest the bran along with the leaves. Bran and cornmeal both expand when they get wet, so when a bran-filled beetle drinks, it pops!

DE-SLIMING Slugs' and snails' wet slimy softness is their weakness. A mulch of finely crushed eggshells, dry sawdust from untreated wood, or a border of ashes will repel them because these fine-grained materials stick to their repulsive little bodies.

A three-inch copper barrier with one inch buried in the soil will keep slugs and snails out of your garden beds. The moist slimy mollusks get an electrical shock when they touch copper.

I Get By with Help from My Little Friends

As they say, many hands make work light, and two heads are better than one. In a garden, many jaws make work light, and many tiny heads are better than one. I am far too large, slow, and clumsy to find even a fraction of the pests in my garden. Luckily, I don't have to. My diverse plantings attract many hungry, helpful critters that are only too happy to search out and digest pests. There is nothing quite so heartwarming as the sight of a truly obese toad living under a potsherd in the vegetable garden; watching midsummer flocks of iridescent dragonflies hawking after mosquitoes is another of summer's great joys. There are many ways to invite small helpers into your garden.

Put Out the Floral Welcome Mat

Indigenous Peruvians plant maize (corn) as a trap crop before they plant cotton. Caterpillars attack the maize, parasites attack the caterpillars, then the cotton gets planted.

Though the larvae of parasitic wasps are carnivorous, and feast upon the soft insides of the hapless beetle larva or caterpillar on which their mother laid eggs, the adult wasps feed on flower nectar. In order to attract gravid females to your garden, it is a good idea to plant nectar plants. Very small, sweet-smelling flowers are the best choice, since these tiny wasps are not strong swimmers and tend to drown in large flowers. Some species of parasitic wasps are incredibly miniscule: braconid adults may be only one sixteenth of an inch long, and some ichneumons and chalcids can be as small as an eighth of an inch. A border of small-flowered herbs like dill, fennel, parsley, and cilantro planted around your vegetable garden will help attract these tiny beneficial insects to your garden. Lower growing sweet alyssum may be planted right in the beds to draw mother wasps directly to the pests on your cabbages, corn, or tomatoes.

Playing Cupid

Many plants cannot form fruit unless their flowers are pollinated. Honeybees and native bees are some of our most valuable pollinators. Encourage them by planting a wide variety of flowers to provide bee sustenance all season.

Both man-made and natural pesticides kill bees far more easily than they kill pests. If you must spray, try to use something nonresidual that kills only on contact, like insecticidal soap or horticultural oil spray.

The very idea of trying to pollinate even a single apple tree by hand exhausts me; I have a hard enough time keeping up with my two tiny indoor Meyer lemon trees!

Offer Them Drinks

Shallow pans of water set in shade will attract insectivores such as ladybugs and toads to your garden. Depending on its species, an adult ladybug can eat between fifty and several hundred aphids every day, and each ladybug larva consumes its own weight in aphids daily. A toad can eat between ten and fifteen thousand insects in a single growing season. No wonder our toads are so fat!

A Home for a Toad

Toads have very simple housing needs. Just a damp bit of ground and a roof over its head and a toad is content. A curved piece of flowerpot on the ground can provide a cozy tile-roofed home for a toad.

Thatched Roofs for Little Helpers

Mulched gardens produce much larger populations of spiders, centipedes, and predatory insects. Ground cover has a similar effect; research has shown that ground covers in orchards improve the quality of the fruit.

After Chinese farmers began building winter housing for spiders in their cotton fields, they were able to reduce their pesticide use by 80 percent. The farmers dig shallow holes, then fill them with grass. These earth-sheltered insulated dwellings help more spiders survive the winter, greatly improving pest control in the farmers' fields. Cotton production elsewhere in the world is dropping steadily as pesticides lose their effectiveness against cotton pests.

Don't overtidy your garden in the fall; fallen leaves and other garden debris can help ladybugs and spiders survive the winter, and toads like to burrow in compost piles to hibernate, so try not to dig into the pile in late fall.

Mosquitoes

The Best Mosquito-Catching Machine in the World

A new type of mosquito-killing machine has recently come on the market. There are several different brands, all of which emit carbon dioxide, heat, and moisture. Female mosquitoes find their prey by homing in on mammalian or avian body heat and exhaled carbon dioxide, so these machines selectively attract the little bloodsuckers. This makes them a huge improvement over brightly lit "Bug zappers" that indiscriminately attract insects, often beneficial ones, and then electrocute them.

The least expensive carbon dioxide mosquito machines cost several hundred dollars, the most expensive over a thousand. Enthusiastic owners' testimonials gush about the new machines: "It killed four to five hundred mosquitoes the first night!" Over the course of a hundred-day mosquito season, one of these machines could conceivably kill fifty thousand mosquitoes, which seems to be a very impressive number unless you look at the competition.

A Look at the Competition

The little brown bat (*Myotis lucifugus*), which is one of the most common bats in the United States, can catch up to seven mosquitoes per minute. This tiny furry mammal, which is smaller than a mouse, consumes between one quarter and one half its body weight in insects, mostly mosquitoes, every night. Over the course of a night it can eat seven hundred mosquitoes—that's seventy thousand mosquitoes in one hundred days. But little brown bats are very gregarious creatures and rarely live alone. A small colony of twenty bats can consume 1.4 million mosquitoes in one hundred days; it would take twenty-eight carbon dioxide mosquito machines to do the same job. If there are already bats living near you, consider yourself extremely lucky.

You may want to erect a bat house to try to lure more bats onto your property. Bats are extremely intelligent creatures, and though attempts to get them to colonize bat houses are not always successful, putting up bat houses is definitely worth a try. Bat houses, like other houses, need to be well-adapted to their climate, so there is no such thing as an all-purpose bat house. Your local Department of Natural Resources or a local wildlife agency may have information about the most effective bat houses for your area. If you can't get information locally, try contacting Bat Conservation International, P.O. Box 162603, Austin, TX 78716. This nonprofit conservation and research organization sells bat houses as well as a book and a video on building bat houses and attracting tenants to them.

Though bat houses are fun, the two most important things you can do to help the bats in your area are: avoid using insecticides, because bats are far more sensitive to chemicals than insects are, and refrain from killing bats when you encounter them.

Bats are more closely related to us than they are to mice, and they definitely do not reproduce prolifically the way rodents do. Most mother bats bear only one baby per year, so killing a few bats can have a big effect on an area's bat population. Before you kill a bat, think about how much its mosquito reduction services are worth.

Though I like bats, and my husband and I have helped quite a few people safely remove them from their homes, I never pick bats up barehanded; I always wear leather gloves. I like chipmunks too, but I would never pick them up barehanded either. One should always be cautious around wild animals.

Mosquito Prevention

If there aren't enough bats in your area, mosquito prevention is probably the cheapest and most effective thing you can do to protect your family from mosquitoes. Mosquitoes will lay their eggs in even tiny amounts of standing water. Patrol your yard, and don't let water sit for more than a couple of days in pet dishes, birdbaths, upturned Frisbees, or plant saucers. Old tires are notorious breeding grounds for mosquitoes. If there is an unauthorized dump in your area where cheapskates abandon their used tires, call your local waste district, explain the situation, and ask if they will waive the normal tire disposal fee so you can clean up the tires without having to pay for the priv-ilege. One year when I rolled forty-four junk tires out of our local woods, the city actually sent a truck to pick them up!

Caffeinated Mosquitoes

Caffeine makes mosquito larvae so uncoordinated that they cannot come to the surface to breathe; put plain powdered coffee or tea in ponds, potholes, and puddles to kill wrigglers. Use just enough of the powder to change the color of the water.

Oiled Mosquitoes

A thin layer of vegetable oil floating on the water's surface will trap and kill mosquito larvae when they come up to breathe.

Weeds, the Other, Slower Pests

The Gentle Art of Botanical Self-defense

A garden can be thought of as an extension or expansion of the gardener's body, and should be treated as such. Just as you would not knowingly infect yourself with a pernicious parasite, you should avoid planting aggressively invasive plants in your garden. Contact your local agricultural extension office to request a list of the noxious weeds and invasive plants that are troublesome in your area. Talk to other gardeners about which plants, cultivated and uncultivated, are bothersome to them. That being said, sometimes it takes awhile for the peskiness of a plant to be recognized, and the general alarm sounded.

Catalogues and garden books may use euphemisms to describe these botanical bullies. Beware of plants whose descriptions include any of the following: instructions on how to eradicate the plant being described, or terms such as "phenomenally fast growth," "tends to get out of hand," "needs control," or "self-sows prolifically." Any tree that is described as fast-growing and short-lived should be considered guilty until proven innocent. So should trees which are described as seeding freely and suckering profusely. Try to avoid infesting your garden with these plants!

Many of our worst weeds were imported as garden ornamentals. Some notorious examples are purple loosestrife, buckthorn, kudzu, water hyacinth, bamboo, St. John's wort, and eucalyptus. These noxious weeds are so rampant that they out-compete native plants, ruining natural ecosystems. Many of them are useless as food sources for native animals, and some are actually toxic; St. John's wort poisons livestock, for instance. If you want to play it really safe, choose plants that have been used in gardens in your area for at least a few decades, then it should be obvious if they are a problem or not.

Though many weeds are annuals or biennials, there are also weedy vines, perennials, shrubs, and trees. These large weeds can cause rather large problems by killing off the native plants that wildlife depends on, and forming large, pure stands that are useless as wildlife habitat. These oversized weeds tend to be rapid growers which spread aggressively, and lead rather short lives. Weed trees often have extremely brittle wood that is useless as lumber, and many are so full of highly flammable oils that they can't be used as firewood. Here is a short list of weedy arboreal invaders:

Common buckthorn (*Rhamnus cathartica,* whose second name refers to the unpleasant properties of its berries) is a small Eurasian native that was introduced to this country as an ornamental. I can't imagine why—it's the ugliest tree I've ever seen. It seeds prolifically and inedibly, and is very hard to eradicate.

Salt cedar (*Tamarix ramosissima*) is another small Eurasian tree that was introduced as an ornamental. It is displacing native plant communities near rivers across the Southwest. It concentrates salt in its leaves, so when the leaves drop, they make the soil salty and inhibit the growth of nearby plants.

Russian olive (*Elaeagnus angustifolia*) is yet another Eurasian small "ornamental" tree that chokes out native riverside plants.

Melaleuca (*Melaleuca quinquenervia*) is a small tree which is native to Australia. It was introduced into Florida in the early 1900s as an ornamental. It was also planted extensively in the Everglades in an attempt to dry them up. Unfortunately, the attempt was almost successful. Melaleuca currently infests over 400,000 acres in Florida, and is so thirsty that it is interfering with water flow in the Everglades.

Blue gum eucalyptuses (*Eucalyptus globulus*) were introduced into California in the late 1800s, billed as "wonder trees," hailed as the perfect lumber trees to replace the nearly decimated redwood forests. In Australia, blue gum provided valuable lumber, but in the less arid California climate the trees grew so full of sap that eucalyptus boards cracked, and eucalyptus railroad ties warped so badly that their tracks peeled off.

Blue gum eucalyptus not only spreads like wildfire, displacing native vegetation, it also fuels wildfires—it is possibly one of the most flammable trees in the world. Eucalyptuses are so full of flammable oil that they don't just burn, they explode. The floor of a eucalyptus grove is also extremely flammable since it is usually carpeted several feet deep with undecomposed leaves, bark, seed pods, and branches. Apparently nothing that lives in California, including the microorganisms, is capable of digesting eucalyptus. Perhaps saddest of all, these gigantic, three-hundred-foot-tall weeds are true to their name, and often fatally gum up the beaks of the hapless birds that attempt to sip nectar from their flowers.

Though kudzu (*Pueraria montana var. lobata*) is a vine, it is also an arboreal invader: it climbs trees and smothers them. Kudzu is a Japanese native that was first brought to the United States in 1876. It was widely planted in the South as an ornamental and a useful and prolific producer of high-quality fodder and hay for livestock. It was also widely planted and promoted by the Soil Erosion Service in the 1930s to stop the expansion of erosion gullies. The Civilian Conservation Corps was enlisted to plant kudzu along roadsides and in gullies throughout the South in the 1940s. By 1955, southerners were beginning to be disenchanted with the miracle plant. None of kudzu's natural enemies had emigrated with it, and it began to be a problem. It can grow up to a foot a day and a hundred feet a year, smothering or strangling whatever vegetation it crawls over. It also breaks off branches, uproots trees and shrubs, and clambers up telephone poles, occasionally snapping them off. It even climbs high-voltage towers and shorts out transformers.

Kudzu has its good points, not least that it makes a wonderful subject for jokes, but it is one plant that probably should have been left home. A single kudzu plant can produce stems as much as four inches in diameter and up to and hundred feet long; its tap root can be more than six feet long and weigh as much as four hundred pounds. This astonishing plant thrives in areas with moderate winters and hot wet summers, and has colonized the East Coast as far north as Pennsylvania.

Flocks of tropical sheep are currently employed in Florida as hooved kudzu killers. Sheep are well known for harming plants by grazing them down to the nubs, and sharp little sheep hooves do additional damage.

Unbalanced Weeds

All of these noxious weeds, large and small, have one thing in common: they became problems after the natural balance was disturbed. Introducing nonnative species into an area that lacks their natural predators is an act of disequilibrium. We should thank our lucky stars that we haven't created more weedy monsters!

Weeds Are in the Eye, and Sometimes Tangled in the Hair, of the Beholder

An article in the March 24, 2001, Lancet *reported that John Stepp of the University of Georgia at Athens and Daniel Moerman of the University of Michigan at Dearborn spent seven months studying medicinal plant use in six isolated villages in the highlands of Chiapas, Mexico. During the study, the villagers collected 103 different plant species that they used to treat a variety of disorders; 33 percent of the medicinal plants were fast-growing plants that thrive in disturbed soil (weeds), though only 13 percent of the plant species in the area are weeds.*

Prevention Failed, Now What?

Weed Out the Weeds' Competitive Advantage

Many weeds thrive on impoverished soils that are deficient in trace elements. Humus is a rich source of many trace elements. Adding humus to the soil helps more desirable plants out-compete the weeds. A heavy mulch will also prevent weed seeds from reaching the ground. The roots of a weed seed that germinates in deep mulch will die of thirst before they can reach the ground.

Changing the pH of the soil will discourage or prevent many weeds. Sheep sorrel, horsetail, and cinquefoil are all signs of acidic soil, and dandelion seeds need acidity in order to germinate. Raising the pH of the soil will discourage all of these weeds. Extremely acidic soil is frequently a sign of poor drainage and a lack of humus. Though spreading powdered limestone or wood ashes on the soil will temporarily change its acidity, adding organic material in the form of well-composted manure or garden compost will be a more lasting solution. It is quite easy to spread a few inches of compost in a flower bed, but lawns should be fed smaller amounts of compost at a time, lest the grass be smothered. An inch of compost can be spread over a lawn and raked in with a leaf rake until the grass blades are above the compost rather than beneath it. If you do this a couple of times during the growing season, your lawn will soon be a marvel of lushness. Every time you pull weeds out of your lawn you should sprinkle a little compost and some grass or clover seeds onto the bare spot. Wandering weed seeds can't germinate unless they land on bare soil.

Carrying a cheese shaker full of grass and clover seed with you when you mow isn't a bad idea either, so you can sprinkle seeds into bare spots whenever you mow over them.

Boiled and Pickled Weeds

A spray bottle filled with equal parts of white vinegar and water is a handy way to kill weeds. The vinegar spray kills weeds most effectively when the offending plant is in the full sun. Aim carefully because vinegar kills weeds and desirable plants indiscriminately. Slugs and snails will also succumb to a vinegar spray.

Boiling water is perhaps the least toxic way to kill weeds. It is especially effective when poured on weeds growing in cracks in pavement.

Killing Trees

Sapling weed trees can be either dug up or pulled out. A locking pliers is a great tool for grabbing and pulling out tiny saplings. Larger trees necessitate a sneakier approach. A good, nontoxic way to rid yourself of mature weed trees is to girdle them. Girdling is when a ring of tree bark is removed all the way around the tree, preventing sap from moving down from the leaves to the roots.

(This technique was invented by rabbits feeding on fruit trees in the winter.) Late spring through midsummer is the best time to girdle trees, as the bark separates more easily from the wood when the sap is flowing. If the tree has tender bark, use a sharp knife to cut all the way through the bark to the wood underneath. If the bark is tough, you will need to cut it with a pruning saw. Peel the bark off between two cuts. The underside of the bark should be green; the green layer is the phloem, which transports the sap from the leaves to the roots. Try not to cut into the wood; cut just the bark and the phloem. If you girdle a tree too deeply and cut into the sapwood, the tree may act as if it has been cut down. Many weed trees will simply resprout if you cut them down, leaving you with many small trees where one once stood. Sometimes new sprouts will even come up from the roots several yards away from the stump. This is not convenient when you are trying to get rid of a tree.

You may want to practice by making parallel cuts a couple of inches long before you begin girdling, so you can figure out how deeply to cut. Once you're done practicing, draw two chalk circles all the way around the tree, an inch or two apart. Cut through the bark using the chalk lines as guides, then peel off the bark between the cuts. If you girdle the tree properly, it will die a slow lingering death over a couple of years, but it serves it right.

Some weed trees, common buckthorn for instance, which seed prolifically, will rapidly ripen a lot of seeds after they have been girdled. If the tree is short enough, you may want to lop off the twigs that are carrying the berries, seeds, or flowers, then destroy them by burning them, letting them rot in water until they're completely gone, or sealing them into black plastic bags to steam in the sun all summer. If you can't reach the seed-laden branches, you may want to spread tarps under the tree to catch seeds as they fall, so you can dispose of them.

When Life Hands You a Lemon...

Look upon gardening problems as puzzles, as mind-enhancing opportunities. Anything that can grow as fast as water hyacinths, kudzu, bamboo, or rabbits could be regarded as a valuable renewable resource rather than as a menace. Water hyacinths not only filter contaminants out of water, they produce a very tough fiber which has been used to make wicker-type furniture in tropical countries. In its native Japan, the rampant kudzu vine is utilized and appreciated. Its vine fibers are made into high-quality paper, its leaves are cooked and eaten, and its roots are processed into food starch.

Rabbits, needless to say, can be eaten. I am sure that many starving people would be overjoyed to have a nice supply of rabbits to eat. How things look depends upon where you are standing while viewing them.

Chapter Seven

Growing Healthy; GARDENING AS EXERCISE

iana Nyad, the well-known long-distance swimmer, wrote an interesting account in her book *Other Shores* about the several months she spent in Africa, training for a long-distance swim. She had been working out all day long every day, and felt she was in the best shape of her life. Near the end of her stay, she decided to attempt to climb 19,340-foot Mount Kilimanjaro.

On the second day of her ascent, she encountered a tiny, frail old woman resting next to her burden by the side of the trail. The old woman's bundle of steel rods and bamboo was bigger than she was. The young athlete decided to see how much weight this ancient woman was carrying, and was shocked to discover that she couldn't budge the bundle.

After a short rest, the old woman picked up her bundle and continued her climb.

When Nyad returned from her successful five-day ascent of the mountain, and made inquiries, she was told that the old woman was employed by the Tanzanian government; she climbed the mountain once a week to deliver building materials to the camp near the summit of the mountain.

Exercise as a Part of Life, Not Apart from Life

For the past twenty years, my main venue of exercise has been the garden, mine and other people's. When I first met my husband, who is seven inches taller than I, I outweighed him! We started an organic landscaping business together, and within a year I had lost thirty-five pounds.

Because of my own experience, I am a great advocate of fitness through work. Many people seem to have trouble sticking with an exercise program. If gardening becomes integral to your life, exercising will not be a burden to you; in fact, when you can't garden, you will feel compelled to exercise, just to use up excess energy.

Most animals love to exercise; just watch dogs running wildly in circles when they are let loose. Our bodies still crave exercise, but our minds, unfortunately for our bodies, rule.

Growing Older and Better

As our dear friend and adopted grandmother Grace says, "You don't get paid well for physical work. Physical work pays off healthwise." She should know: she's in her mid-eighties and still mows her own lawn, shovels her own snow, and can easily outwork people half her age. "Longevity takes physical work," she says. "Work will keep you young."

Grace views everything as an exercise opportunity: a pile of gravel, a pile of compost, snow, a longish lawn, autumn, a friend to visit, a dirty carpet. If she's home, a neighbor's newly delivered truckload of topsoil, gravel, or sand never fails to draw her outside, shovel in hand, eyes sparkling, ready to help.

Grace makes sure she gets some exercise every day: if she can't garden, walk, shovel snow, clear brush, rake leaves, or mow, she goes down to the basement and walks her treadmill, rows her rowing machine, twists on her twisting board, and rides her stationary bicycle. When I see mice in pet shops busily running on their exercise wheels, they remind me of Grace.

While collecting material for this book, I interviewed Grace over her Scrabble board, while sharing many pots of tea. Grace grew up on a farm and really knows how to work. She also knows how to play: she knows a game for every possible occasion (Easter egg rolling is my favorite); she's still pretty good with a hula hoop and a jump rope, and she wins about 90 percent of our Scrabble games.

But "work and accomplishing something is my fun," says Grace. "I try to accomplish one thing a day and then I can be pretty happy." Playing is fun, but working is *really* fun. Hindus believe that there are many paths to enlightenment. One of those paths is through work; though she is not a Hindu, I believe that is Grace's path.

Slow and Steady Wins the Race

Scientists are just starting to figure out what Grace has known for years. The U.S. Surgeon General's *1996 Report on Physical Activity and Health* concluded that accumulating thirty minutes a day of moderate activity, such as gardening, can help people maintain a healthy weight and reduces the risk of many chronic diseases, including heart disease, type-2 diabetes, hypertension, and colon cancer. A study published in the *Archives of Internal Medicine* in April 1999 showed that the cardiac benefits of an hour of moderate exercise are equal to the benefits of an hour of strenuous exercise.

Moderate exercise may actually be healthier than strenuous exercise. In the early 1980s, an English immunologist named Lynn Fitzgerald began training for competitive long-distance running, and found that her health was deteriorating. She investigated, and found signs of immunodeficiency in many highly trained athletes, including herself. She concluded that though moderate exercise is known to strengthen the immune system, overly strenuous exercise may compromise it.

Researchers have also discovered that aerobic fitness is based on the total amount of work you do, not how long it takes to do it. This is very good news for people who wouldn't dream of "exercising" for four, five, or six hours at a time, but will happily garden all day long.

Moderate exercise is exercise that can be sustained comfortably for at least an hour. Gardening and walking are considered moderate exercise, but consult your doctor before exercising if you are sedentary.

A Lean, Green, Gardening Machine

Researchers have also discovered that people lose more body fat when they work out at a slower pace than when they work out more intensively: walking a mile in eighteen to twenty minutes burns up more body fat than walking a mile in fifteen minutes. Fat is a very efficient fuel, but burning fat requires more oxygen than burning carbohydrates does. It turns out that the most efficient way to burn off body fat is to exercise moderately, not strenuously, and the longer the better. Walking a mile at a moderate pace will burn off more fat than running a mile. Exercising at a low intensity for more than ninety minutes is apparently the optimal way to burn fat.

Gardeners tend to putter around their gardens for extended periods of time, far longer than it would be possible to exercise anaerobically. I have often noticed, while harvesting autumn leaves for my compost, that though at first leaf-raking seems effortless, after a few hours of raking I find myself panting as if I had just run a race.

A 160-pound non-elite runner who finishes a marathon in four hours uses up about 3,000 calories. That same person would burn up more than 2,100 calories during six hours of light gardening such as weeding and pruning. Not impressed, you say? But what is that non-elite runner doing the day after the marathon while the gardener is happily puttering in her garden?

Healthy Right Down to the Bones

Dr. Lori Turner, an associate professor of health sciences at the University of Arkansas at Fayetteville, studied the effects of various forms of exercise on the bone density of women aged fifty and older. She discovered that only weight training and gardening helped these women maintain a healthy bone density. The other activities she studied—calisthenics, bicycling, swimming, jogging, and walking—did nothing to prevent osteoporosis. Weight training and gardening are both weight-bearing activities, and bones become denser when they support more weight.

There is a big difference between a working body and a modeling body. Hard work tends to build up muscle. A working body will look very different from a model's body, but hardworking muscles and bones will be strong and healthy. I look forward to the day when good health becomes the standard for beauty.

Each fall for the past five years my husband has done a pruning job for a retired physician whose wife decided she didn't want her husband to get up on the garage roof anymore to prune their huge apple tree. The doctor is now in his eighties.

While I was gathering material for this chapter, I asked the doctor what he thought about work as exercise. He said that he grew up on a farm in Iowa, and his Saturday morning chore had been to churn eight pounds of butter. "We used up eight pounds of butter a week!" he marveled. He estimated that his parents ate between five thousand and six thousand calories per day; both lived into their nineties, and were slim their whole lives. Today, the average American eats between two thousand and three thousand calories per day.

Americans keep trying to figure out the right diet for people who do no physical work. In March 2001, the Centers for Disease Control and Prevention announced that only a quarter of all American adults got enough exercise in the 1990s. Almost 30 percent of Americans reported that they got no exercise at all.

Especially when I am gardening for myself, gardening is not about speed, it is about pleasure. So timesaving machinery is irrelevant: I do not find enjoyment in engine noise and exhaust fumes, and I get a great deal of pleasure out of manual labor.

There are definitely jobs that are best done by machine; one must be flexible and allow for this. For instance, felling large trees is more safely done with a chain saw than with an ax or a two-person saw. My husband is the one who does this in our family; my job is to pull on the guide rope, or if my services are not needed, I can stay in the house and cower and pray. I'm terrified of chain saws!

Sometimes the availability of machinery induces people to do more work than is necessary or useful. For instance, we never rototill an area before landscaping it, thereby sparing ourselves days of unpleasant, noisy, wrist-numbing labor, as well as saving clients the extra expense.

I once had a homeowner return from doing errands and ask me what machine I had used to level out the humps in his front yard. "Me," I replied: I had leveled the area with my pet pick-mattock.

There are, of course, some instances where a small front-end loader may be necessary, but usually I have managed without one.

Gardening is more like a dance than a race. Garden at a slow, steady pace, and you will be able to work all day, and the next.

Gardeners, like dancers, need to be strong and flexible. Gardening will help make you strong, but flexibility is generally something that must be worked on. Stretching before and after gardening can help prevent muscle soreness. Stretch slowly, and don't bounce; bouncing can cause tiny tears in muscles. Hold all stretches for at least thirty seconds.

Pregardening Stretches

RAG DOLL STRETCH: The purpose of this stretch is to loosen up your spine. Bend over slowly, rolling down "vertebra by vertebra."

Bend over as far as you can, let your head and arms dangle loosely. Move gently and let them swing a bit. Slowly roll back up to a standing position.

NECK STRETCH: Nod slowly and exaggeratedly a couple of times. Yes! Yes! Yes!

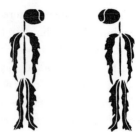

HEAD TURNING: Look left, then right, and repeat a couple of times. No! No! No!

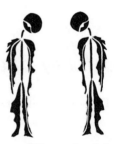

SIDEWAYS NECK STRETCH: Tilt your head slowly, right ear to right shoulder, then left ear to left shoulder. Repeat.

NECK ROLLS: Roll your head slowly, one way, then the other. Repeat.

SHOULDER STRETCH: Shrug your shoulders as high up as you can, then push them down as low as you can.

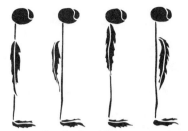

SHOULDER CIRCLES: Circle shoulder one way, then the other. Switch sides.

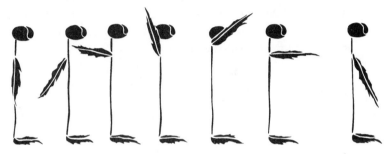

ARM CIRCLES: Windmill your arm forward a few times, then backwards. Switch arms.

ARM STRETCH: Pull your arm across your chest by gently pulling your elbow with the other hand. Switch arms.

BACKWARDS ARM STRETCH: Clasp your hands together behind your back, lift them as high as you can, then bend over from the waist.

THIGH STRETCH: Bend your right knee and reach behind you to grasp your right ankle. Stand up straight, and pull your foot up as close to your gluteus maximus as you can. This will stretch the quadriceps muscles along the front of your thigh. Hold this stretch for at least half a minute. Repeat with the other leg.

LEG STRETCH: Stand facing a wall. Place your palms on the wall at shoulder height. Position your feet so your arms extend straight out, and your feet are shoulder width apart. Keeping your feet flat on the floor, bend your elbows and lean forward until you feel a nice stretch in your calf muscles. Hold this stretch for a minute or more.

Now go garden!

Stretch Your Back While You Garden

When our friend Al, a physical therapist, reviewed this book he insisted I include this exercise: Unless you are a gymnast or a dancer, most of your daily work involves bending forward, not bending backwards. Think of your spine as being built like a stack of alternating blocks of wood (vertebrae), and soft jelly doughnuts (discs), which you want to keep in good shape. When you bend forward, the soft discs tend to compress in front and bulge out toward the back of the spine, where the nerves live.

BACK STRETCH: If you remember to stand up, put your hands on your hips, and bend backward, every ten minutes or so, you will alleviate the pressure on the back of the discs and help prevent sciatica, lumbago, slipped discs, and plain old back pain. (*Note:* Al's wife, Theresa, who is the gardener in the family, laughed when Al said to stand up and stretch every ten minutes.) Most gardeners get too engrossed in gardening to remember to stretch that often. Stretch as often as you can.

Don't forget to take time out to lie on your back in the grass and watch the clouds.

Postgardening Stretches

BACK-RELAXING STRETCH: Lie on your back on the floor, with your arms by your sides. Bend your knees and pull your feet as close up to your derriere as you can. Flatten the small of your back down to the floor. Keep your knees together. If this seems difficult and uncomfortable, get up and go find an old necktie or scarf. Lie back down and tie your knees very loosely together with the necktie. This will help your back and legs relax.

Now cross your arms over your chest as far as you can. Just lie there for as long as you can. As you relax, your back will relax, your crossed arms will cross farther and farther, and your hands will droop closer and closer to the floor. The first time you do this stretch, it probably won't feel as if anything is happening, but if you wait long enough, your back will start to ache, and then make soft cracking noises, and suddenly feel wonderful. The more often you do this stretch, the more quickly it will work. The first time I did it, it took me half an hour. When I got good at it, a couple of minutes in this position would make my back crack.

Even if you do no other stretches with your gardening, you should still do this one. For many years it has kept my back pain-free and healthy.

Follow the previous stretch with the following:
Lie flat on your back on the floor, and stretch your right arm out on the floor above your head, but out at a diagonal, as if you are doing half of the YMCA song at a baseball game. Stretch your right leg out over your left leg, but close to the floor. Now stretch your right arm and right leg out simultaneously so that you get a nice, diagonal pull. Repeat on the left side.

Energy Conservation

Try to use the least possible amount of energy to do any given job—this means your energy or a machine's. The less energy you use, the less damage you are doing to the environment.

Minimize the amount of work you have to do by letting materials do some of the work for you: shade out and kill weeds or sod by smothering it with mulch, cardboard, or a thick layer of composted manure. Heavily mulched perennial beds rarely need weeding, and the weeds that do manage to come up are quite easy to pull out of soft, well-mulched soil. Double-digging or rototilling your garden beds will be rendered unnecessary if you simply shovel a thick layer of well-aged manure or compost on top of the beds and plant right into it.

Plant Power

If the weight of heavy machinery has created a compressed, bricklike layer of hardpan in your garden space, you can break it up by utilizing the tremendous power of plants' roots. Plant annuals or biennials with deep taproots. The deep roots will break right through the hardened layer, and when the plants die, their roots will add organic matter to the soil. Alfalfa, lupines, and many different types of clovers all work well for this purpose.

Energy Conservation Is Very Important

Sit down on the job as much as possible, preferably in the shade or under a beach umbrella. Smell the roses, play with toads, listen to warblers, watch dragonflies, admire spiders, laugh at chipmunks, and throw sticks for your dog.

Sitting down while gardening brings you very close to the action; you may end up nose to antennae with pests. If you encounter pests, kill them by hand and take responsibility for it: squash caterpillars, blast aphids with a spray from the hose, spray vinegar on slugs, swat mosquitoes.

Try to avoid kneeling for long periods of time. It's hard on the knees. Squatting is better if your knees are strong, but it may take a bit of getting used to. It is very easy to fall backwards out of a squatting position if you are not accustomed to it. Squat with your feet flat on the ground and very far apart. If squatting is too difficult, try kneeling with only one knee down; use a kneepad and alternate sides frequently.

When squatting or bending over, stand up frequently and stretch, or you may find it difficult to straighten up at the end of the day.

A Healthy Gardener Is a Well-Watered Gardener

Hard work and sweat go together like Mary and her little lamb. In very hot weather it is quite easy to become dehydrated if you do not make an effort to drink a lot of water. Some days the recommended eight glasses is enough; other days it's two gallons. If you're not sweating, drink more!

Sodium is lost through sweat, and when sodium levels drop, excess potassium is excreted. Then, if the body's sodium level is raised through the ingestion of typically salty American convenience foods, the potassium levels will remain low. Potassium depletion may lead to muscular weakness, cardiac abnormalities, and edema (the accumulation of fluid in the body's tissue).

Unless you have a medical reason to keep your potassium levels low, it is a good idea to eat potassium-rich foods if you are working hard and sweating a lot. Avocados, bananas, orange juice, and baked potatoes are all high in potassium. We also put "lite" salt in all our salt shakers (half sodium chloride, half potassium chloride), and it helps.

And While We Are Sweating

Birgit Schittek and her colleagues at the Eberhard-Karls-University in Tübingen, Germany, reported in 2001 that they had discovered that human sweat contains an antimicrobial protein, which they dubbed dermicidin, that acts against a wide range of pathogenic organisms and may help stave off infection. Dermicidin is expressed only in sweat glands, where it is secreted into sweat. It proved remarkably effective against Escherichia coli, Enterococcus faecalis, *and* Staphylococcus aureus. *The protein also exhibited strong antifungal capabilities, killing the yeast* Candida albicans. *The authors concluded that dermicidin "may help limit infection by potential pathogens in the first few hours following bacterial colonization."*

One stinky hot, humid day, my kids were helping me on a landscaping job, and I learned a valuable lesson. I had sent them into the shade to work, while I worked in the sun. Soon they were complaining that they were too hot. I was horrified when I realized that it was actually more uncomfortable where they were working than in the full sun, because the trees were holding heat and humidity down close to the ground. We went home after having worked only two and a half hours.

Very heavy gardening is no different from any other strenuous physical activity: in order to stay healthy, you may need to alternate the intensity of your workouts. If you garden very strenuously one day, you may need to do lighter gardening or none at all the next. When you are tired, stop. In my entire landscaping career, I have never managed to work longer than six hours in a day.

Some people work best later in the day; our friend Jim does most of his garden work at night. Everyone is different. Garden when it pleases you to garden.

Though the Puritan work ethic would have us believe that only laziness keeps people from starting work early in the morning, sometimes working in the morning is not a good idea at all. In hot weather, follow the shade, and drink lots of water. If the shade comes around at three in the afternoon, start then.

If you are not capable of a lot of hard physical labor, there is nothing wrong with hiring, asking, or bartering for gardening help. But you can still participate. Sit under a tree or an umbrella near where your helper is working. Talk to your gardening friend, exchange gardening and design ideas; carry weeds to the compost pile in whatever way you can: wheelbarrow, sack, wagon, wheelchair. Gardening is too much fun to miss out on. Make sure to have your paths made accessible.

Heat, humidity, smog, altitude, and cold all affect how hard we can work. In some instances, it is best to take the day off. When you work hard, and breathe more deeply and rapidly, the carbon monoxide from car exhaust and from other sources of combustion tends to concentrate in your blood, so try to avoid working outside on smoggy days.

Make your contribution to cleaner air by planting smog-tolerant deciduous trees on weekends when there is less traffic and less exhaust. The formation of photochemical smog increases as temperatures rise. Trees are the best air cleaners we have: they reduce smog by lowering temperatures around them as well as by absorbing carbon dioxide. Trees also absorb and break down other air pollutants, including nitrogen dioxide, ammonia, sulfur dioxide, carbon monoxide, ozone, and particulates.

The Exercise Habit

Because I am so accustomed to doing physical work all day, I did most of my reading and note-taking for this book while walking on an elliptical trainer. I noticed an interesting phenomenon while doing so: if a book was interesting and well written, I could "ride my machine" for hours; if the book was badly written and boring, I would only last about fifteen minutes on the machine before I felt exhausted and had to lie down. Boredom is exhausting. Perhaps that is why so many exercise programs fail.

Chapter Eight

Tools and How to
USE THEM

sing your mind before you begin using your muscles can greatly increase the amount of work you accomplish, and decrease the amount of work that needs to be redone.

Books are tools at least as much as shovels and saws are. In fact, books are more important. One can work with no tools at all—pulling weeds, moving rocks—but gardening without any information is futile.

A basic garden library should include: a good general gardening book, for instance one of the Sunset Gardening Books; a well-illustrated pruning book; an insect identification book; and a weed identification book. Experienced gardeners will be happy to recommend good regional gardening books.

My husband, who loves to prune fruit trees and shrubs, looks up the proper procedure for each species each fall before he does any pruning. It is very easy to forget the details over the course of a year. A branch cannot be reattached once it has been pruned off. Read twice, prune once.

The Gardening Body

Though gardening can make one feel extremely strong, healthy, and invulnerable, human bodies are easily damaged by sudden encounters with hard, heavy, fast-moving, or sharp objects. The appropriate safety equipment should be worn whenever there is the slightest possibility of serious injury. We are probably the most likely to have accidents when we are in too much of a rush to put on the proper safety equipment.

It is very important to obey the safety warnings on tools, no matter how silly they may seem. I once gave myself a black eye while loading staples into a staple gun; I was extremely lucky I didn't blind myself.

How to Prevent Accidents and Injuries

Avoid putting objects on top of ladders.

Don't leave garden rakes on the ground with the tines up; put the tines down, and step on the rake's head to push the tines into the ground.

Don't leave saws or blades of any kind where they can be tripped over or banged into. Don't leave pruners open.

Don't work in the hot sun. In fact, if you can avoid it, don't work at all in very hot weather.

Every job takes longer than you think it will. This is mostly a problem if you are trying to estimate a job for someone else. You will never get as much done in a day as you had planned. Don't rush to finish a job. Haste makes waste and causes accidents.

Garden-Tool Maintenance

Well-maintained tools are safer than neglected ones:

Put your tools away clean; scrubbing them down every once in a while with steel wool soaked with vegetable oil doesn't hurt either. Sandpaper your tools' handles when they get splintery.

Paint your tool handles with easily visible fluorescent paint. Brown- or green-handled tools are very easily mislaid.

Keep your edged tools sharp by using a file or a grinding wheel on shovels, hoes, and spades, and a whetstone on the outside edge of pruners and loppers.

The Well-Dressed Gardener Wears Protective Clothing

The gardener's body is her most useful and versatile tool and should be carefully protected. Appropriate clothing and protective gear are extremely important to a gardener's health, comfort, and safety.

Necessity is the mother of invention, but experience is its costumer. When I "helped" our neighbors with their haying this summer, I had everything I could think of that I might need: long sleeves, long pants (predirtied), and a straw hat held on with a chin strap. But having never hayed before, I was unprepared for the huge amounts of chaff that blew into my eyes. After only two and a half hours on the wagon (which, coincidentally, was about how long it took me to acquire "wagon legs"), I had to quit, because my eyes were streaming tears and I couldn't stand the pain any longer. Next time I will bring goggles, and a bandanna to cover my mouth and nose.

The Gardeners Tool Box

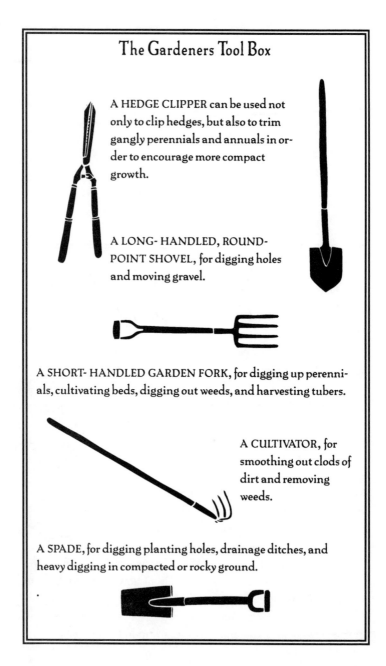

A HEDGE CLIPPER can be used not only to clip hedges, but also to trim gangly perennials and annuals in order to encourage more compact growth.

A LONG- HANDLED, ROUND-POINT SHOVEL, for digging holes and moving gravel.

A SHORT- HANDLED GARDEN FORK, for digging up perennials, cultivating beds, digging out weeds, and harvesting tubers.

A CULTIVATOR, for smoothing out clods of dirt and removing weeds.

A SPADE, for digging planting holes, drainage ditches, and heavy digging in compacted or rocky ground.

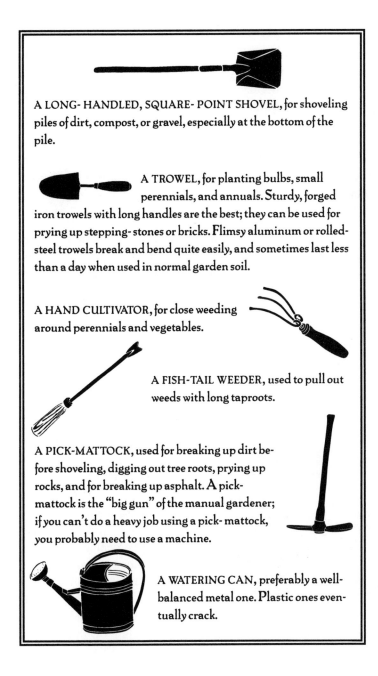

A LONG- HANDLED, SQUARE- POINT SHOVEL, for shoveling piles of dirt, compost, or gravel, especially at the bottom of the pile.

A TROWEL, for planting bulbs, small perennials, and annuals. Sturdy, forged iron trowels with long handles are the best; they can be used for prying up stepping- stones or bricks. Flimsy aluminum or rolled-steel trowels break and bend quite easily, and sometimes last less than a day when used in normal garden soil.

A HAND CULTIVATOR, for close weeding around perennials and vegetables.

A FISH-TAIL WEEDER, used to pull out weeds with long taproots.

A PICK-MATTOCK, used for breaking up dirt before shoveling, digging out tree roots, prying up rocks, and for breaking up asphalt. A pick-mattock is the "big gun" of the manual gardener; if you can't do a heavy job using a pick- mattock, you probably need to use a machine.

A WATERING CAN, preferably a well-balanced metal one. Plastic ones eventually crack.

I don't need to be a fashion plate while gardening. I have been with Prince Charming for over twenty years, and he is not particularly interested in how I look in clothes. He also doesn't seem to know the difference between his going-out-to-dinner clothes and garden wear, and will, if not prevented, pull weeds or dig while dressed up.

Gardening garb is not necessarily appropriate for any other known human activity; mine has been known to induce both hilarity and incredulity in friends and neighbors. I have a few definite objectives in mind when I dress for a day's gardening. Starting from the feet up:

FOOT PROTECTION: I keep my feet dry and relatively mud-free. Leather footwear, which lets the feet breathe, is best for gardening. In dry weather, leather tennis shoes work fine for doing light gardening. Heavier gardening requires heavier footwear. Leather work boots with a stiff shank and a reinforced toe protect arches from shovel pressure, and toes from errant picks, rocks, and wheelbarrows.

Heavily textured waffle soles trap and hold a lot of dirt, so choose a boot with the shallowest tread you can, unless you are working on very steep slopes. Knee high rubber boots are necessities for wet weather gardening. Rubber boots with steel reinforced toes and steel shanks are available.

SUN AND INSECT PROTECTION: : Sometimes I lie awake at night

trying to figure out new ridiculous gardening outfits with which to amuse my friends. On more than one occasion a friend clad in shorts, sandals, and a T-shirt has laughed hysterically at the sight of me in my gardening clothes.

My normal summer gardening costume includes: an unbuttoned light-colored cotton long-sleeve shirt worn over a cotton T-shirt, light-colored cotton pants, and a wide-brimmed straw hat with a chin strap, sometimes with a kitchen towel clothespinned to the back to keep the sun off my neck. I may look hotter, and definitely more ridiculous than my friend, but given the same sun exposure, I will stay much cooler. When I am doing sit-down gardening, I often stick a beach umbrella in the ground so I can work in the shade. This has started a minor fad with farming friends.

HAND PROTECTION: Well-fitted gardening gloves are a necessity. Lightweight cloth gloves are fine for pulling weeds, but leather gloves are the best choice for heavier jobs. Gloves prevent blisters and sunburn and provide protection against thorns, stickers, broken glass, and the occasional enraged ant. It is a good idea to wear gloves even if you're only going to pull out a couple of weeds before you go out to dinner; I have managed to get "papercuts" from stiff blades of grass on more than one occasion.

When a Rock Lands on a Finger, Too Bad, Too Bad for the Finger

Building rock walls is an interesting and amusing pastime, but rocks are completely unforgiving, and gardeners must be careful and deliberate while doing rock work.

It is very easy to damage your fingers horribly when building rock walls. Some friends of ours, who used astonishingly large (up to five-hundred-pound) rocks to hand build ten-foot-tall retaining walls in their steep little hillside yard, broke a finger apiece.

Protect your fingers from rocks by wearing heavy-duty leather gloves, and avoid putting your fingers between a rock and a hard place (use wedges). If a top face of a rock has a projecting point or edge, break it off before setting the next rock on top of it. I like to wear extra big gloves I can slide out of easily if I need to. You can even pack some dirt in the gloves' fingertips to protect your own. Dirt-packed glove tips protect the gardener's fingers in exactly the same way as pointe shoes protect a ballerina's toes, though the gloves are far less dainty.

EYE PROTECTION: Always wear safety glasses or goggles when pruning, hammering, using an ax, hitting rocks or concrete with a sledgehammer or a pick, using power equipment, or using a staple gun. Safety goggles with mesh "lenses" don't steam up in hot weather. A mesh face shield or mesh goggles can make seeing a little more difficult, but getting whipped in the eye by a twig can make it hard to see for the rest of your life.

Dancing with Tools

Gardening shouldn't hurt. Work movements, because they are repeated so often, can eventually become refined and dancelike. Keep your back straight, your weight over your hips, and your feet about shoulder distance apart. Don't rush. Give yourself time to establish a rhythm.

Tool dancing, like many other forms of dance, depends more upon leg and footwork than upon arm movements. You hold your partner in your arms, and the power and impetus come from your legs. Even when I'm using a pruning saw, I try to brace my arms against my body and use my legs for some of the power, otherwise my work day is sure to be quite short, probably less than an hour.

Tool Cheating, or How to Look Stronger Than You Really Are

Years of trying to keep up with my larger, stronger husband on landscaping jobs drove me to develop "cheating" techniques to make up for my comparative lack of upper-body-strength.

Normal leg muscles are far stronger than arm muscles. Whenever possible, use the power of your legs rather than your arms. Not only will you be able to accomplish more, you will put far less strain on your back.

When you must use your arm muscles, try to keep your arms as close to your body as possible. This puts less strain on your joints. Bend over from your hips, not from the middle of your back.

Shovel Cheating

Lift shovel loads with your legs. Let the shovel handle rest on your thigh—when you are lifting the shovel, your thigh will act as a fulcrum. Your thigh may get a bit bruised if you do a lot of shoveling, but your back will thank you.

Two Loads Are Better Than One

Make several light trips rather than one heavy one. You may pay dearly for the time you save by making one heavy trip. When you are carrying things—say, watering cans—try to carry one in each hand. An even load is easier on your back. Whenever possible, use a wheelbarrow or garden cart instead of carrying items in your hands.

Leg Lifts

When you are lifting heavy objects, lift with your legs, not with your back. If at all possible, try to avoid lifting those heavy objects. The easiest way to move rocks is to roll them backwards between your legs, and if possible, downhill!

How to Lift a Large Rock Using a Wheelbarrow

A good heavy-duty large-capacity contractor's wheelbarrow makes a very effective rock-lifting tool. The tub must be made of steel and have straight sides so it can lie flat on its side on the ground.

Rock lifting with a wheelbarrow is a two-person job:

Tip the wheelbarrow on its side. Roll the rock into the bucket of the wheelbarrow.

The two rock movers stand on

opposite sides of the wheelbarrow. The worker on the wheel side puts his foot on the uphill leg of the wheelbarrow, and holds on to the uphill side of the bucket with both gloved hands; he is the Puller. The worker on the bucket side puts one hand on the uphill side of the wheelbarrow, and the other hand on the rock; he is the Pusher.

Working together, the Puller pulls on the uphill side of the wheelbarrow while stepping down heavily on the wheelbarrow's uphill leg, meanwhile the Pusher pushes on the rock and the uphill side of the wheelbarrow. The Pusher should stay alert and be ready to jump back if the wheelbarrow slips or the rock starts to roll out of the wheelbarrow.

When the wheelbarrow is upright, center the rock in its bucket to balance the load. It will be easier to roll the wheelbarrow if the load is toward the front, over the wheel.

We have been using the same wheelbarrow since we began landscaping. It is so beaten up from the tons of large rocks that we've dumped into it over the years, that one lady who saw it sitting in our yard mistook it for a garden ornament and asked where I had found the quaint antique wheelbarrow. With great difficulty I managed not to laugh as I replied that it was new when we bought it.

Rock'n' Roll

Be careful going downhill with a wheelbarrow: a heavy load can put an enormous strain on your back. Garden carts can be especially dangerous on hills; they are so well balanced that you may not realize how heavy the load is while it is on level ground.

Tone Your Thighs as You Trim Your Woods!

It may seem a bit macabre to mention that you can whittle away excess flab on your thighs while using a lopper, but it's true.

Removing a small sapling is generally much easier with a lopper rather than a pruning saw, but the strength required to use a lopper is proportional to the diameter of the wood you are cutting. Because I am a bit lazy, I have figured out how to augment the strength of my arm muscles, enabling me to avoid some sawing—I use my legs. This method should only be used to remove unwanted plants or to renew overgrown shrubs— lilacs for instance— by cutting the thick old branches back to a few inches above ground level. This technique is not to be used for precision pruning.

Position the lopper's jaws around the sapling or stem. Do a deep knee bend and brace your knees up against your forearms.

Squeeze steadily with your arms and legs until you cut all the way through the sapling or stem.

There is a well-advertised bit of exercise equipment that works on the same principle as my lopper cheating method: put the handles between your thighs, and squeeze.

Selecting the Right Tool for the Job

Choose the heaviest tool you can comfortably use for any given job. The weight of the tool will do a lot of the work for you. The right tool for any given job depends upon the size and strength of the gardener, so choose your tools based on your own size and strength.

A carpenter's hammer is no substitute for a sledgehammer when pounding in stakes, and using a spade to dig up a perennial is easier on the wrists than using a trowel for the same job.

Use a long-handled lopper instead of hand pruners to prune anything larger than twigs. After years of using scissors or a knife to cut pumpkins and winter squash from their vines at harvest time, I finally figured out that the best tool for the job was a far larger one: a long-handled lopper.

My favorite tool is a pick-mattock with a five-pound head. I refer to it as my pet pick-mattock because it is the tool I use most frequently: I most often use the mattock end in the same way as a dog digs a hole, moving material from the front to the back. I use it to clear and level ground, break up sod, move large rocks, hack out tree roots, and root out weeds. Though using a heavy tool requires exertion on the upstroke, the weight of the tool does most of the work on the downstroke. A light tool is easier to lift, but requires hard work on the downstroke. I can happily use my pick-mattock all day long, but using a hoe quickly exhausts me.

Garden tools that feel comfortable to the individual user are the right ones to use. The cool-looking "modern ergonomic" ones may not suit at all. I snapped the tip off a fancy aluminum trigger-gripped trowel while prying up a flagstone at our first job, but I didn't really mind because the darn thing gave me blisters.

When buying new tools, it is generally a good idea to get the best ones you can afford. The first garden-forks and shovels we bought lasted less than a month. We're still using the heavy-duty ones we replaced them with.

Sometimes the right tool is an odd old one picked up at an estate sale. Keep your eyes peeled for the deceased's favorite tool. This tool is more likely to be heavily worn from sharpening, to have a modified or shortened handle, and to be significantly lighter than when it was new, due to heavy use. If you find a tool like that, *buy it!* My second favorite tool, after my pet pick-mattock, is our friend Jim's sawed-off, short-tined garden fork. It is a sit-down tool that I can use while working under my beach umbrella. The handle is short because Jim sawed it off after it broke, and the tines are short because they have been worn down.

There are advantages to having a few beat-up tools that can be used for gritty jobs: a dull old lopper that shouldn't be used for precision pruning can be used to cut roots out of planting holes, and so can a dinged-up ax. This is much easier than cutting roots with a shovel or spade, and much preferable to ruining a good lopper. Sand, dirt, pebbles, and rocks will all ruin the cutting edge of a good lopper or ax.

Don't Let Those Trees Knock You Around

If you are cutting large branches or trees, wear the appropriate safety gear, which is: a hard hat with a mesh visor or goggles, good work gloves, and steel-toed boots if you have them. If you're using a chain saw, you should also wear chain saw chaps and ear protection. If you don't already own all the appropriate safety gear for tree work and chain saw work, you are probably inexperienced in this realm, as I am, and you would be well advised to hire a professional tree service to do your heavy tree work. Tree work is extremely dangerous, and I would not advise anyone who is inexperienced to attempt it.

If there are dead, rotten trees on your property, and you want to knock them down, look up. If the tree is big enough to hurt you if it lands on you, *do not push or kick it over. Tie a rope around it and pull from a distance.*

Any tree that is rotten enough to be pushed over by a human is rotten enough to snap off halfway up as well as at the bottom. The top piece frequently snaps off before the bottom does, and will not go in the direction you are pushing the trunk; it will fall straight down and hit you on the head. A young friend of ours knocked himself out that way a few years ago.

Chapter Nine

Is It Useful, or Is It DECORATIVE?

 **any, if not most, garden elements have** origins that are not purely decorative. Because gardening is a sideline for most of us, we assume that it has always been that way. It hasn't. The vast majority of people throughout history had to work hard to produce their own food, clothing, and shelter, and tended to spend their time as productively as possible. The plants and objects that made up the earliest gardens were certainly beautiful, but being decorative was probably not their main function.

The first pergolas—cross pieces and rafters laid across columns— were used to hold up grapevines in ancient Egypt; arbors were a latticed elaboration of pergolas. The earliest garden statues were religious in nature and depicted deities; they were sacred images that were worshipped in public and private religious services that were often conducted in gardens in ancient times.

The first cultivated flowers were actually culinary and medicinal herbs. Madonna lily (*Lilium candidum*), autumn crocus, water lily, and bluebells are a few of the common garden flowers which began as medicinal herbs in ancient Egypt, and roses were grown for perfume making long before they were used as ornamentals. By the year 1700 B.C. there were seven hundred herbs in the Egyptian pharmacopoeia.

Some Misunderstandings Are Funny

Heavy round stone disks with holes in the middle, which had lain in display cabinets for years in the Santa Barbara Museum of Natural History, labeled "ritual objects," were relabeled after a visiting fisherman identified them as net weights. There are a vast number of "ritual objects" out there, just waiting for someone to identify them correctly. Many things may appear purely decorative simply because we have forgotten their utilitarian origins.

Some Misunderstandings Are Tragic

The island of Bali became part of the archipelago nation of Indonesia in 1947, when Dutch colonial rule ended. In 1965, the Indonesian government, advised by European agricultural scientists, began an enthusiastic campaign to increase rice production, and wholeheartedly embraced the new rice-growing technologies of the "Green Revolution."

Bali, which was one of the most productive rice-producing regions in Indonesia, was one of the first targets of the Green Revolution. Bali's beautiful irrigated rice terraces had been astonishingly productive throughout more than a thousand years of continuous cultivation. All other systems of irrigated agriculture in the world have eventually declined due to loss of soil fertility and the buildup of salts in the soil. Mesopotamia, the world's first civilization, collapsed when its soil became too salty to support plant life. Soil degradation caused the decline of classic Greek civilization and probably contributed to the fall of the Roman Empire.

Despite the astonishing productivity and stability of traditional Balinese agriculture, however, Western consultants were confident that they could improve upon the Balinese system.

Only half of Bali's streams and rivers flow during the dry season. The system that had enabled Balinese farmers to maintain such high productivity depended upon a complex system of religious ceremonies and intermeshing calendars which coordinated farming activities such as water distribution, crop planting, and pest and disease control with a degree of precision and delicacy unmatched anywhere else in the world. Farmers and priests cooperated in ceremonies held in "water temples" every 105, 210, or 420 days; the intervals between ceremonies were tied to the 105-day growing period of native Balinese rice.

During these water temple ceremonies, farmers, elected at the local rice-roots level by farmers whose fields were irrigated by the same canal, worked with priests to set the calendar for each field under the jurisdiction of that Water Temple: when the field would be flooded, when it would be drained, and when it would be planted. Pest control measures that either starved, drowned, or burned pests were coordinated for all the fields in a particular area, ensuring the best possible control.

Heads of the Water Temples climbed their mountain once a year to represent their Water Temple at an annual ceremony held at the Mountain Temple for their district. Leaders determined the ritual cycles for the whole watercourse at the Mountain Temple ceremony, staggering the planting schedules and optimizing water use for the whole district.

Leaders from the Mountain Temple then advanced to a ceremony at one of three Master Water Temples to further coordinate agricultural schedules. The highest level of planning occurred at the two Lake Temples located at the high mountain lakes that feed all the rivers in Bali. The Lake Temple ceremonies coordinated all the agricultural activity on the island.

When the Green Revolution was inflicted upon Bali, the Indonesian government implemented new agricultural policies to promote continuous cropping of hybridized high-yielding rice varieties that required the use of chemical fertilizers and pesticides. In the 1970s, farmers were forbidden to plant the slower-growing, less-productive native rice varieties and bureaucrats usurped control of the irrigation and cropping patterns from the Water Temples. A government banking system was set up to provide credit to small farmers to buy chemicals and machinery.

Water shortages and plagues of rice pests and diseases followed the Green Revolution like gadflies after a cow. Rodents and insects flourished due to the uninterrupted food supply. The soil became harder to plough, the supply of irrigation water became unpredictable during the dry season, and productivity declined. District officials began to report "chaos in the water scheduling" and "explosions of pest populations."

The first variety of hybrid rice, IR-8, was designed to thrive when fertilized with chemical fertilizers and protected with pesticides. By 1977, almost 80 percent of South Central Bali's terraces were planted with IR-8, which turned out to be highly susceptible to the brown plant hopper, which destroyed 2 million tons of Indonesian rice that year.

So the rice scientists developed another hybrid, IR-36, which was fast maturing and resistant to plant hoppers. The new hybrid was susceptible to tungro virus, which decimated the rice crop in 1983 and 1984.

A tungro-resistant hybrid, PB 50, immediately succumbed to Helminthosporium oryzae, a fungal disease.

When farmers wanted to return to the Water Temple system of irrigation scheduling, the foreign consultants at the Bali Irrigation Project assumed they were displaying religious conservatism. Because the Balinese agricultural system predates modern science, its technical terms are symbolic. The agricultural consultants misunderstood the role of the religious symbolism inherent in Balinese agriculture, in which a Goddess inhabits the sacred mountain lakes from which the irrigation water flows; gods inhabit irrigation dams and springs; the Rice Mother is incarnate in the growing crop; and plague-bearing demons from the sea are responsible for agricultural pests and diseases.

Traditional Balinese agriculture depended upon intricately intermeshed irrigation and planting schedules which were coordinated using ceremonial painted wooden calendars to keep track of ten different weeks ranging in length from one to ten days. Symbols inscribed on the calendar enable the user to keep track of all ten weeks and the way they intersect. The calendar helps mark out multiple intervals of any desired length up to 210 days, which was the length of the entire rice cycle of Old Balinese Rice. During the Water Temple ceremonies, the calendar is set for the interdependent farmers and their fields.

Far from being a quaint display of religious piety, the Balinese Water Temple system precisely coordinated the agricultural cycles of growth and decay all over the island. Rice grown in terraces is planted in flooded fields, which are kept flooded for most of the 105-day growing cycle. Flooded fields grow blue-green algae, which supplies nitrogen to the rice, and fish, which supply protein to the farmers. Gradually the depth of water is decreased, until harvest time, when the fields are dry. Wild grasses are allowed to grow after the harvest, and are ploughed under just before the next cycle begins. The deep-rooted wild grasses draw nutrients up from the subsoil, making them available for the next crop of rice.

By 1991, the Balinese government had seen enough of the effects of the Green Revolution to issue the following statement: "In response to the threat of severe toxic contamination from pesticides and gradual loss of soil fertility, the government of Bali now strongly supports the use of traditional techniques of coordinated fallow periods as the primary method of pest control."

Luckily, many farmers whose remote fields were far up the mountainsides, and less likely to be raided by government officials, had clandestinely continued to plant the native Balinese rice varieties. Their stubbornness saved these beautifully adapted varieties from extinction.

Ancient Balinese religious texts stated that neglecting the Water Temples would lead to the spread of pests and diseases and loss of the water needed to make crops grow. The ancient texts were obviously written by people who knew what they were talking about. Why try to argue with success that has lasted over a thousand years?

Given the long history of civilizations declining along with their agricultural productivity, I find it astonishing that the Green Revolution "scientists" could have stood and gazed with dry eyes upon an agricultural system like Bali's, and believed they could improve upon it; I would have been on my knees, blinking back tears.

Increasingly salty soil is currently threatening agricultural productivity in the San Joaquin Valley of California, in the Rio Grande Valley, and in the Indus, Nile, Murray-Darling, Jordan, and Tigris-Euphrates River valleys. Perhaps teams of Balinese farmers and priests could be sent to these areas as agricultural consultants.

Up on the Living Roof

Tenochtitlán, the capital city of the Aztecs, was described by the conquistador Hernan Cortez, who could certainly not have been accused of being sensitive, as looking like a flower garden. The roofs of all the houses of this city of 700,000 were so thickly planted with flowers that from a distance they gave the impression of being giant flower beds; the streets looked like garden paths. "Hanging gardens" stretched between the houses. Yet all this beauty did not prevent Cortez and his soldiers from razing Tenochtitlán and building Mexico City on its dust.

There is nothing new under the sun: contemporary versions of the Aztecs' roof gardens are springing back to life in modern cities.

Modern cities, with their vast acreage of pavement and flat gravel or black tar roofs, soak up huge amounts of heat during hot summer days. On such a day, the temperature on a gravel roof can be up to 45 degrees Fahrenheit (25 degrees Celsius) hotter than the ambient air temperature. This means that on a lovely 80-degree summer day, the temperature on a flat gravel roof could reach a balmy 125 degrees Fahrenheit. The cumulative effect of all these impermeable surfaces increases city temperatures by several degrees; urban planners have dubbed this phenomenon the "urban heat island" effect. Thus begins a vicious cycle: higher urban temperatures increase the demand for electricity to run air conditioners, leading to an increase in the production of carbon dioxide and other pollutants which increase the earth's ambient temperature, creating further demand for air-conditioning.

Just as sweating cools the human body through evaporation, plants cool the air as water transpires through their leaves. A single large tree has the cooling power of five average-size air conditioners. But unlike air conditioners, which create more heat as they run, trees decrease overall city temperatures.

Roof gardens can be established on flat roofs using potted trees, shrubs and other plants, or they can be planted completely with grass or other ground covers. Roofs that are completely grass covered, though not common, are beginning to be built on urban buildings throughout Europe. Because grassed roofs have better insulating properties and smaller temperature fluctuations, they last longer than conventional roofs.

Green roofs can absorb between 50 and 100 percent of the precipitation that falls on them in the summer, and between 40 and 50 percent of winter precipitation. This impressive reduction in runoff helps reduce erosion and pollution in the local watershed. Conventional roofs, unless they are rotting, absorb zero percent of the precipitation that lands on them.

Green roofs can also absorb and filter out many common urban air pollutants such as carbon dioxide, which is largely responsible for global warming, and sulfur oxides and nitrogen oxides, which are major components of acid rain. And of course, plants produce the oxygen that we all so enjoy breathing. The more plants growing in an urban area, the better.

Plants growing up the sides of buildings can provide many of the same benefits as roof gardens: better air quality, shade, and reduced building temperatures.

Since Mexico City is now blessed with some of the worst air in the world, perhaps it is time to reinstate the Aztecs' flowering climate control and air purification system.

Computer models created at the Lawrence Berkeley National Laboratory in California show that large numbers of roof gardens could reduce urban temperatures by as much as 5 degrees Fahrenheit. Germany and France have already provided incentives for their urban citizens to plant roof gardens; Swiss municipalities are encouraging the planting of existent flat roofs, and in Bern, a law has been introduced that would require planted roofs on all new construction as well as on all buildings undergoing renovation; Chicago's Mayor Daley has authorized funds to build a roof garden on top of City Hall, and is strongly encouraging Chicagoans to plant roof gardens.

Note: The roofs of single-family dwellings may not be strong enough to sustain the weight of a roof garden. Please check with a structural engineer before proceeding. All roof gardens require specially formulated lightweight planting mixes.

If Truth Is Beauty, and Beauty Is Truth, What Is a Parking Lot?

No one could possibly argue that "utilitarian architecture," like that of gas stations and shopping malls, with their flat roofs and acres of parking lots, is beautiful. Planting strategies that help ameliorate the dismal environmental effects of these horrible constructions could only improve them. (If you are an architect who designs these monstrosities, I humbly request your apologies.) Every time I pass these "contributions" I dream of how they could be:

Imagine a shopping mall that is roofed with flowers, trees, and grass and embellished with a living facade of plants; its climate control system lollygagging along at half speed or less.

Think about its parking lot, divided by vegetated swales which help slow down and filter runoff, so nearby creeks can run cool and clean. Every parking spot is shaded, not only because of the trees but also because of the vine-covered pergolas that roof the entire parking area. In snowy climates, the pergola roofs are made of retractable wires, which can be rolled up for the winter to facilitate snow removal.

The "modern" design movement, which pioneered the use of exposed pipes as decorative elements, was supposedly based on the idea that form follows function. Unfortunately, they were right. Ugly form follows badly integrated function. Environmental costs need to be factored into our design decisions. Beauty is not superfluous; it is actually a fairly accurate gauge of how well things fit together.

> "When I'm working on a problem, I never think about beauty. I think only how to solve the problem. But, when I have finished, if the solution is not beautiful, I know it is wrong."
>
> —R. BUCKMINSTER FULLER

Ornamental Pest Control

Blowin' in the Wind

Wind chimes and bells have been part of many world cultures for millennia. Bells are commonly hung from temple roofs in many Asian and Southeast Asian countries, including India, Tibet, China, Japan, Bali, and Burma. The chimes are believed to scare away evil spirits.

Small pieces of metal striking together, like those in wind chimes or bells, emit ultrasonic squeaks as well as the sounds we can hear. Some of these sounds are in the same range that bats use for echolocation. A wide variety of night-flying insects, including katydids, crickets, locusts, praying mantises, green lacewings, beetles, and moths, are able to hear bats echolocating. Ultrasonic sounds send panicky insects into bat avoidance dives.

Hanging chimes in your trees may scare away more than evil spirits.

Confuse-a-Pest

Japanese gardens often feature picturesque winding or crooked paths. These paths are crooked not simply because they are prettier that way but because the Japanese believe that evil spirits travel in straight lines and will be unable to negotiate bent paths. There may be more than charming superstition to this belief. Insect pests do travel in straight lines. Crooked paths are not conducive to the straight line plantings that encourage pests.

Reflections of a Confused Pest

Researchers have proven that a reflective mulch of aluminum foil disorients moths, aphids, and thrips and prevents them from landing. If you don't fancy the look of aluminum foil in your ornamental garden, you might try placing a few gazing balls in strategic locations, for instance near your prize rosebushes.

Gazing balls, which go in and out of gardening fashion because it is so hard to decide whether they are cool or kitchy, have been around for at least seven centuries. Whether or not they repel witches, ill fortune, illness, or evil spirits as they were designed to do, they are almost certain to disorient and repel insects that are confused by reflective surfaces.

A Hedge Against Pests

Many woody herbs with strongly scented leaves—lavendar, santolina, and hyssop for instance—emit volatile oils which strongly repel insect pests. Many of these plants have traditionally been used to make the beautiful small clipped hedges that form the intricate designs in "knot gardens." Every time these hedges are clipped, they increase their production of aromatic oils.

Flying the Yellow Banner of Pest Control

Many insect pests are helplessly attracted to the color yellow. Yellow sticky traps, which are usually stiff yellow cards coated with a nondrying sticky adhesive, but which can actually be any yellow object with stickum on it, exploit pests' fondness for yellow.

A few years ago, Peruvian potato farmers began walking up and down in their fields, carrying yellow banners. Though it looked as if they were participating in a parade, what they were actually doing was decimating the potato pest population in their fields. The yellow banners were coated with a sticky adhesive. The farmers were participating in an Integrated Pest Management Program that was designed to kill insect pests that had become resistant to chemical pesticides, and allow beneficial predatory insects to recover from decades of pesticide use.

Continuity

Home landscaping is not an industrial process, and that is exactly why so many of us love to garden. Many of the gardening technologies of preindustrial people are still as relevant as they were when they were first invented. Trying out "new" old ideas is one of the great pleasures of gardening.

Chapter Ten

The Meditative GARDENER

he path is an ancient metaphor for the
soul's journey through life. Misdirected lives are
compared to confused paths; upright lives are
described as straight, shining paths. Anyone
who has ever been lost in a wilderness area will
have a vivid understanding of the importance of clearly marked
trails. (I was, and I have.) A well-defined path is a wonderful thing.

The nucleus of the Japanese tea garden is the path that leads
from the house to the garden pavilion where the tea ceremony is
held. The plantings are designed to be viewed from the path.
Walking in the tea garden is meant to be an aesthetic, meditative
experience that augments the experience of the tea ceremony.

Though the danger of becoming seriously lost is minimal in
most gardens, garden paths are still quite important; they guide
people where you want them, and away from where you don't
want them. Strategically placed paths can help steer walkers away
from the root zones of sensitive trees, and tough walking surfaces
can help protect the ground from erosion.

Though many people happily walk mazes, thereby traveling
nearly the longest possible distance between two points, the public
has a general propensity for shortening distances by "cutting
across." You can lead a man to a path, but you can't make him

walk on it. Because of this, many garden designers wait to see where the shortcuts are forming, then pave the shortcuts.

Following the garden path is as pleasant a way to go through life as I can imagine. If you truly aspire to follow in the tortured footsteps of Ernest Hemingway, Sylvia Plath, Vincent van Gogh, or Kurt Cobain, perhaps you should stay out of the garden, for fear of dissolving your artistic angst. Gardening is an art that tends to induce serenity (perhaps van Gogh should have grown *Artemisia absinthium* instead of drinking it).

The Zen of Puttering

Concentrating on an interesting and complex task can make the hours fly by like minutes. Artists refer to this state of consciousness as "flow," and many athletes refer to it as "being in the zone." The timeless feeling of "flow" is what keeps gardeners puttering all day long in their gardens, day after day, and has inspired countless plaques, tiles, greeting cards, and stepping stones inscribed: "One is never so close to God as when one is in a garden."

Communing with God in a garden is not a recent phenomenon. In Genesis, God created man and immediately planted a garden to put him in. In ancient Mesopotamia and Egypt, China and Japan, the earliest gardens were laid out and planted by monks. In ancient Greece, gardens evolved from sacred groves; they were used as places of public worship and were tended by priests.

Buddhist texts tell us that the young Prince Siddhartha, who was to become the Buddha, first experienced meditation while sitting under a rose-apple tree (*Syzygium jambos*). He had accompanied his father to a ploughing festival, and the plight of the worms and the other small creatures that were cut by the plough had aroused his sympathy. He sat in the shade of the rose-apple tree to think and entered a state of deep meditation.

When Prince Siddhartha was a young man with a wife and infant son, he left home to seek enlightenment. He became a monk, and wandered in search of spiritual masters. He studied sitting meditation with various masters for several months at a time, learning to reach higher and higher states of consciousness.

After several years of meditative studies, he decided to try to reach enlightenment through asceticism. He practiced extreme austerities for six months, until his hair was falling out in clumps and his skin hung on his bones. Then, while sitting in meditation in a cemetery, he remembered the first time he had sat in meditation, as a boy under the rose-apple tree, and he realized that mind and body are connected, and to abuse the body is to abuse the mind. He used this experience to formulate the Middle Way, the path to enlightenment which avoids the extremes of both overindulgence and self-denial.

Siddhartha resolved to gain back his strength, and abandoned his attempt to escape the phenomena of the world. He began eating and drinking normally again and began practicing walking meditation. He began meditating on natural phenomena—bird song, sunlight glowing through a leaf—and realized that each breath, each small step, everything he encountered, were all part of the path to liberation.

When he had regained his strength, the former hermit sat down on a cushion of newly mown hay under a peepul tree (*Ficus religiosa*) and resolved to meditate there until he attained enlightenment. He sat in the lotus position for a whole day and night until the next night, while armies of demons and devils unsuccessfully tried to distract him. He reached enlightenment, then sat under the tree for another week. He had become the Buddha, the Enlightened One. The peepul tree became famous as the bodhi (awakening) tree, or bo tree for short.

While the Buddha was meditating, he realized the interdependence of all phenomena; the stars, the trees, and the universe itself were meditating with him, and he felt at one with the thousands of insects, birds, and animals that shared the forest with him.

All this is very similar to the natural meditation that any child, or lucky adult, can achieve in the shade of a tree. But of course the Buddha went much farther than that, and went on to found one of the great religions of the world. The depth of his experience exceeds that of the casual meditator under a tree as the ocean exceeds a drop of water.

Garden Meditation

The Garden of Eden was not the House of Eden, and Paradise is described as a garden. I think it is no coincidence that Prince Siddhartha became the Buddha while meditating under a tree. Sir Isaac Newton "discovered" the law of gravity while under a tree (how else could an apple have fallen on his head?); Gregor Mendel invented the science of genetics while experimenting with his peas; and Charles Darwin's garden had a "Sand-walk," where he walked in circles every noon while he thought, refined arguments, and refuted counter-arguments.

Every time I have attempted sitting meditation, legions of anti-meditation demons have assailed me. But even the Buddha enjoyed walking meditation. I do working meditation.

Repetitive tasks can be quite meditative. I hate to blow my own horn here, but I am capable of having a perfectly empty head all day long while gardening. At other times sudden thought strikes like lightning. For instance, last summer while scything the path through our woods, I suddenly understood for the first time the metaphor of the Grim Reaper. The scything mentality is relentless and remorseless. Anything in the way comes down, whether it is grass or small saplings.

I believe that a well- loved garden can be an external manifestation of the gardener's mind, a visible, living dream.

Our friend Eleanor is one of the most spiritually active people I have ever met: always reading, thinking, talking, attending lectures, and experimenting in her garden. Eleanor is a master gardener for

our county; other master gardeners in the program get misty-eyed when they talk about visiting her garden. It is not a fancy garden, but it produces tranquility more prolifically than a zucchini plant produces zucchinis.

Eleanor grew up on a farm in Edmonton, Alberta, and now lives with her husband and son on Connemara, a small farm on Island Lake, about five miles from our house. Eleanor, though in her early eighties, is always willing to try something new, never assuming that she knows a subject already. Though she knows a lot about gardening and farming, she is always eager to learn more.

Eleanor cultivates experience as avidly as she cultivates beans. "Along with knowledge comes insight and understanding. Be open for any little insight that comes your way. If you have a closed mind, all kinds of knowledge will float right past you," says Eleanor. She also stresses the importance of reading and learning from other people's experience: "I don't say it isn't real if it hasn't happened to me."

Once, while Eleanor was deciding which perennials needed to be dug out of one of the flower beds, she said, "You can't have everything at once; you have to get rid of some stuff," then laughed, because, like most farms, Connemara is full of stuff. She added, "We are so tied up with material things; we're so happy when we get things. And I have so much stuff and I don't know how it got here!"

One of the many charming "things" on the farm is a tiny old house that stands at the edge of the asparagus patch. Its front wall is missing, and shelves of old bottles and a few old tools line its walls. The missing wall makes it look like an enormous dollhouse.

Empty Mind, Full Soul

The purpose of sanctuaries, according to the late mythologist Joseph Campbell, is to induce a state of mind that is not centered in the self. In India, this state of mind is known as "the other mind," or "absentmindedness."

Often while I am digging and hauling, my mind goes curiously blank. My body does the thinking, and my thought processes become very large and visible to the naked eye, as easy to read as the thoughts of a column of food-laden ants traveling back to their hill.

After one particularly long day of shoveling and wheelbarrowing compost, moving rocks around, planting potatoes, mulching with hay, pine needles, and wood shavings, harvesting worm compost and planting irises, it occurred to me that gardening can largely be a matter of moving things back and forth. We gardeners might as well be a really gigantic species of ant. A solitary ant is really not a viable organism at all, and possesses no more intelligence than a single disconnected transistor on a computer chip, but a colony of ants is more like a fully functioning computer processor. The combined efforts of many gardeners, all working on similar problems and sharing information, make us an extremely powerful human computer. Millions of us, thinking, pondering, meditating as we trundle about our dearly beloved gardens, can be a dynamic and positive force in the world.

How to Keep All Your Marbles

Recent research suggests that elderly people whose daily lives are physically active have healthier brain function than their more sedentary contemporaries. Eleanor would laugh at the thought of working out in a gym; doing her chores is plenty of exercise.

Plant Twelve Petunias and Call Me in the Morning

Depressed people are four times more likely to die from heart disease than are non-depressed people. Dr. Dominique L. Musselman and colleagues at Emory University in Atlanta, Georgia, drew blood samples from depressed and non-depressed subjects to try to discover why. They found that depression increases the stickiness of blood platelets by 41 percent. These abnormally sticky platelets are more likely to cause blood clots in the blood vessels.

A 1999 study conducted by Bruce McEwen and Firdaus Dhabhar at Rockefeller University showed that chronic, long-term exposure to stress hormones can damage neurons in the hippocampus, the part of the brain which is critical to memory and learning.

Researchers at Duke University Medical Center compared the effects of exercise and antidepressants on depressed elderly patients. They found that though exercise took longer to start working, after four months of treatment, exercise was just as effective as the medications at relieving depression. These formerly depressed patients also showed improvements in memory, planning, organization, and multi-tasking. According to researcher James Blumenthal: " The implications are that exercise might be able to offset some of the mental declines that we often associate with the aging process."

Gardening, Mental Exercise of Champions

The world is such a complex place that we are constantly bombarded with more information than we can process. In order to prevent sensory overload, we pay no attention to most of this input, because if we did, we would rapidly go mad.

But the same mechanism that enables us to block out unimportant information can endanger the health of our brains. Research has demonstrated that novel experiences stimulate the brain to grow new connections between different areas of the brain. The brain can ignore predictable, expected information, like that generated by following a routine. The more routine our lives are, the less mindful we are of our lives, and the less mind we will eventually have.

Gardening is a wonderful way to learn through experience, annually. I relearn the same things every year: the winter is so long that to my chagrin, every spring I have trouble recognizing weeds and perennials as they come up.

I love the intellectual challenge of a good juicy gardening problem; so I start a lot of projects just to see if I can make them work. Luckily, I am really good at making mistakes, because if by some miracle I ever did something the right way the first time I tried, I would have absolutely no idea why it worked. If the goal of man is knowledge, I am reaching my goal via the path of maximum mistakes.

Vita Sackville-West, the English novelist, poet, and gardener extraordinaire, wrote: "Gardening is endlessly experimental, and that is the fun of it. You go on trying and trying, testing and testing, and sometimes you have failures but sometimes you have successes which more than make up for the failures."

Though by day's end I might not remember what I ate for breakfast, I always remember what small furry creatures I crossed paths with in the garden, what butterflies flitted past, what I planted, and what I carried.

To Sleep! Perchance to Dream and Think

For millennia, dreams have been recognized as a different way of thinking and a path to inspiration. According to anthropologists, before the advent of modern lighting, people commonly slept in two nightly phases of four to five hours each. Shortly after midnight, people commonly awoke for one or two hours and talked about their dreams.

Moderate physical fatigue, as opposed to mental or emotional fatigue, is blissful. One of gardening's better features is that it is physically tiring. Being tired is a wonderful way to resist watching large amounts of unnecessary late-night television. I strongly believe that the time I spend dreaming is some of my most valuable time.

Many people consider sleeping a waste of time, and use caffeine as a means to decrease the time they spend asleep. Scientists are currently at work on a drug that enables people to avoid sleeping at all. Needless to say, the military is vitally interested in this research. The very thought of not sleeping horrifies me.

I have always needed more sleep than average, but I don't mind anymore, because I have finally accepted the fact that I do my best thinking in my sleep. A very large percentage of this book was written while I slept: when I awoke in possession of material for the book, it would have to be transcribed before I got up, lest getting out of bed derail my train of thought. I believe that when I go to sleep with a question in my mind, my subconscious attacks the problem from every possible angle.

The ability to solve a problem doesn't necessarily depend upon how much intelligence one brings to a given problem. How long one brings intelligence to a problem may be more to the point. I am not the fastest problem solver in the world, but I am extremely persistent, and if I persist, I often reach my goal.

One of my favorite dream anecdotes is the story of how the nineteenth-century chemist Friedrich August Kekulé figured out the structure of benzene. He had been working on the problem for a long time, with no success. But one night he dreamt of snakelike objects twisting and turning, then suddenly, "One of the snakes had seized hold of its own tail, and the form whirled mockingly before my eyes." When Kekulé awoke, he realized that the benzene molecule formed a ring. Before Kekulé, chemists had thought that it was not possible for humans to discover the structure of molecules.

Kekulé was able to dream the answer to the puzzle of benzene because it was a problem he desperately wanted to solve, and he already possessed the knowledge he needed.

Don't Get Up Yet!

Samuel Taylor Coleridge apparently composed his poem "Kubla Khan or, A Vision in a Dream," while napping. He reported that he fell asleep in his chair while reading about Kubla Khan, awakening three hours later with a poem, which he believed to be two or three hundred lines long, complete in his mind. He immediately began writing it down, and had completed the first fifty-four lines when he was called out for an hour on business. When he returned, he discovered to his chagrin that the memory of the rest of the poem had melted away. "Kubla Khan" is only fifty-four lines long.

Gardening Advice: To Take It or Not to Take It, That Is the Question

I have learned from gardening, life, and elder friends to listen and hear and digest what is being said to me. And if the speaker is someone I trust and love, I digest their knowledge and learn from it. I do not dismiss it as harebrained, wacky, or clichéd. The simplest, most beautiful explanation is usually the best one, the working version.

I must insert a caveat here about gardening advice: since I believe with all my heart that my duty is to my planet first and foremost, the gardeners whose advice I take without reservation are organic gardeners, who do not use garden poisons of any kind.

Can a Garden Think?

It seems that there may be a lot more to listen to in a garden than we thought. Evidence of sentience seems to be cropping up everywhere these days.

Scientists led by Toshiyuki Nakagaki of the Bio-Mimetic Control Research Center in Nagoya, Japan, found that the shape-changing slime mold Physarum polycephalum *was able to negotiate a five-inch-square maze. Though in the absence of food the organism's body covered the entire surface of the maze, when food was put at the entrance and exit to the maze the slime mold reconfigured to cover the shortest possible distance between the two food deposits.*

A slime mold is a single-celled fungus that exhibits properties of both plants and animals. Some slime molds look like smears of jelly, while others have phases that look like vomit. Having encountered many a slime mold, it is astonishing to me that anyone could have had the imagination and insight to test one in a maze.

What else is thinking out there?

Multitudes of people have passed this way before, many of them extremely successfully, emotionally and spiritually. They have left numerous hints, clues, anecdotes, and stories behind. Much of their wisdom has been turned into clichés, because an idea that has been useful tends to be repeated often. "God helps them that help themselves," wrote Benjamin Franklin in *Poor Richard's Almanac* in 1757, but the ancient Greek hero Hercules said it first.

Getting good advice is important, but we must then decide what to do with it.

The Mind Waves, and Matter Waves Back

Physicists conducting experiments in quantum mechanics have repeatedly observed phenomena which suggest that the experimenter's expectations affect the behavior of photons. According to quantum physics, photons of light are waves and/or particles, but humans can only observe them in one form at a time, either as a wave or a particle.

There is a quantum mechanics experiment in which photons are beamed toward a screen with two slits in it. An observer behind the screen is equipped with a system that can detect either the interference pattern that appears when a single photon travels in wave form through both slits, or the photon passing in particle form through a single slit. When the observer tries measuring the photon in wave form, the photon is always found in wave form. When the observer tries measuring the light in particle form, the light is always in particle form. This phenomenon has led some physicists to wonder whether photons possess consciousness. It makes me wish my dogs were as well behaved as photons.

In *Onward and Upward in the Garden*, Katherine White remarked that plants she didn't like seldom thrived in her garden. If photons seem to exhibit consciousness, why shouldn't plants?

My husband and I once prevented an oleander bush from growing for a whole year. Oleanders are so incredibly poisonous that people have died after using the sticks to roast hot dogs. A client wanted an oleander in her yard, and though we were terrified that a vulnerable member of her family would taste the oleander and be poisoned, we could not convince her that an oleander was a bad idea.

We planted the shrub in as inaccessible a spot as we could find. It was on the same irrigation system as all the other plants in the yard, and we didn't do anything to it physically, but we hated it. After a year, the oleander had not grown even a centimeter, and everything else in the yard was looking gorgeous, so the homeowner allowed us to rip the poisonous thing out.

Anyone who doesn't believe that the human mind is powerful should try growing some plants. Like photons in a quantum physics experiment, plants tend to do what we expect of them. Perhaps people with "green thumbs" truly believe that their plants will thrive, so they do. People who claim to have "brown thumbs" don't expect their plants to thrive and the plants often prove them right.

Don't Give Up Till the Roots Rot Out

When I was a young girl in California, a hard frost killed one of our young orange trees. My mother sawed it off, leaving a foot-high stump. Ten years later the orange tree suddenly put out leaves and began to grow again. Though frost had killed the top, its roots must have been fed by the roots of the orange tree next to it.

Last spring a friend discovered that one of her climbing roses had been girdled at ground level by rodents and looked completely dead. She told her husband not to bother putting the rose's trellis up, because it was dead. By summer, when I saw the rose, it had sprawled in red and white striped glory all over its bed. Its trellis was still in the garage.

Seeds can wait for years before sprouting, trees and shrubs are frequently resurrected, disconnected bits and pieces can grow into whole new plants.

> "It ain't over till it's over."
> —YOGI BERRA

A Watched Flowerpot Never Blooms in Time to Impress Visitors

You had better garden to please yourself, because gardens are very much like small children and dogs: when you want to show them off, they tend not to cooperate. A garden's moment of perfection will seldom occur while visitors are there to be impressed: something will have fallen over or have been eaten in the interim. Gardening is really a private pleasure that can never be experienced as strongly by a visitor as by the gardener herself. Vanity in a gardener can be a fleeting and risky business.

The Joys of Serendipity

Mother Nature has far more tricks up her sleeve than we can possibly imagine. I can't even fathom how big her sleeve might be.

Last fall half a dozen pine siskins perched on the lip of one of the rain barrels near the bird feeder, drinking out of the barrel. This is what makes gardening so wonderful: I am not in control, I didn't order pine siskins, I didn't even know what they were until I looked them up.

The Garden of Bliss

My garden is part of me, and I am part of my garden: I have contributed sweat, food, energy, and a little blood now and then, when I have been careless. The product of all this effort is such overwhelming joy that it makes me laugh at the slightest provocation.

Let'em Laugh

Neuroscientists have found that when research subjects look at a stereoscopic display that shows each eye a different picture, they see one picture, then the other, not both at once. This phenomenon is called the binocular rivalry phenomenon. Neuroscientist John D. Pettigrew discovered that when people laugh, this rivalry between the right and left sides of the brain disappears. A laughing subject whose right eye is shown vertical stripes while the left eye is shown horizontal bars, will see both at once. (Does this mean they see plaid?) Laughter, according to Pettigrew: "rebalances the brain, and literally creates a new state of mind." The belly-laugh effect lasts up to half an hour.

Last summer our puppy somehow got the hanging hook of a vacationing houseplant caught in her collar. That purple Wandering Jew really wandered, all over the yard at a very high rate of speed several times, shedding bits and pieces of leaves, until the pot finally disintegrated in a flower bed on top of a flattened sunflower. How could we not laugh?

Squeeze as much enjoyment out of your garden as you possibly can. Break out those funny books and fake noses. Put up a squirrel-go-round. Lie down on the grass and tickle each other. Squirt each other with water bottles. Laugh at toads, they don't mind. Life is too serious to be serious.

Gardening in Circles

It becomes very obvious, once one has been a gardener for a while, that chaos is very real: everything is very obviously interconnected. No matter how straightforward a garden chore may seem, it is virtually impossible to do one job at a time. Moving a single bag of leaves may necessitate building housing for a toad which has suddenly become homeless. Bringing home a perennial from a friend's house may necessitate relocating three other plants in order to make room. A rake's handle may need to be sanded before a vegetable bed can be readied for peas. I suppose I might find this annoying if I didn't think it was so funny.

This reality is the only reality I know: striped hummingbird moths hovering near sweet peas; a doe and her twin fawns hesitating at the edge of the lawn in the morning; the loyalty of dogs; beans breaking their poles with the weight of their produce; vivid orange sunsets; dew-spangled spiderwebs; fuzzy baby phoebes wobbling in their nest; fat, sticky frogs; and a family to share all these wonders with.

May your garden be well looked after, and well loved, may the rain that falls on it soak in and stay clean, may you enjoy the company of many different plants, animals, and people, and may your garden make your life more comfortable.

Chapter Eleven

In CONCLUSION

hatever other sins of omission and commission I may have committed in writing this book, I hope that I have largely avoided being boring. Gardening, and gardening books, are supposed to be fun, otherwise why bother?

Organic landscaping requires only a few simple rules. Once you understand the rules, everything else flows from them. The rules I garden by work very well for me, and work well for other people, but everyone is different. Experienced gardeners eventually build up their own styles and systems of gardening, because gardening is a way of life, and we must all eventually make our own way.

About twenty centuries ago in Rome, Columella wrote: "the husbandman should be attentive to the instructions of those who have gone before him... such writers serve rather to initiate the workman in his task, rather than to render him expert in it. For experience is the cardinal point in all practical matters... knowledge is to be acquired even by our very failures."

A century ago Vita Sackville-West wrote: "then I rebelled, as all good gardeners should rebel when they find their own experience going against the textbook."

Gardening books are useful tools, not religious texts.

An Active Mind Is the Best Labor-Saving Device

The aboriginal people of Australia's Southwest Kimberly coast used simple, stable rafts made of two sections of lashed and pegged mangrove poles. The rafts were not propelled: the people relied on their knowledge of the tides to travel between offshore islands. I'd like to learn how to garden that way: to know the currents (not currants, though they are nice too) of my garden so well that I can confidently navigate them, with my most advanced technology being that which is between my ears, and that which sits on my bookshelves.

Enduring beauty is a sign of balance and good health. We turn toward beauty just as surely as sunflowers turn toward the sun; it is in our nature to do so. When a beautiful area is made ugly, you can be sure that it is no longer environmentally healthy. Many cultures that are very close to the earth worship beauty; for instance, the indigenous Japanese Shinto religion began as an agricultural rice-growing religion. Shinto shrines are built wherever people have been inspired by a sense of wonder and awe: near a venerable old tree, an impressive rock, a waterfall, the ocean, or a beautiful view.

Oddly, some of the same words that describe beauty and pleasure also describe hunger: ravishing, delectable, delicious, satisfying, and feast. Is it possible that in order to be happy, one must work up a hunger? A garden can satisfy physical and aesthetic and spiritual hunger while inducing physical hunger. But exposure to beauty can also induce hunger for more beauty; gardeners tend to be greedy for more of their favorite colors, smells, and tastes.

My garden has given me turtles; nesting birds; toads; bats flying at dusk; beautiful iridescent bodied, black-winged damsel flies; fireflies; butterflies; baby phoebes with fuzzy little heads the size of viola petals in a nest over our back door; mama and papa phoebe playing in the sprinkler in the garden; baby spiders filling the midribs of a large dandelion leaf; toads hopping on paths, across the lawn, hiding under flowerpots and mulch; tree frogs swimming in water barrels, and bivouacking under the cover of the propane tank; chance seedlings; and new color combinations I would never have thought of by myself.

Love in our garden means strawberry kisses, dandelion crowns, and new rosebushes brought home like trophies. Children's contributions include peeled twig trellises, photo documentation of the garden (with costuming), extra fancy bean poles, wildlife announcements, singing while weeding, and, last but not least, the teenaged boy's version of brush clearing: climbing a sapling, then riding it to the ground as it breaks.

Designing and planting a personal paradise is as much about process as it is about product; the process is never-ending, the product and the process are one. For a true paradise gardener, bliss arrives with dirty fingernails and muddy knees.

BIBLIOGRAPHY

Aldington, Richard, and Delano Ames, trans. *New Larousse Encyclopedia of Mythology.* New York: Crescent Books, 1989.

Arrington, Leonard J., and Davis Bitton. *The Mormon Experience; A History of the Latter Day Saints.* New York: Alfred A. Knopf, 1979.

Bailey, L. H., and Ethel Zoe Bailey. *Hortus Second; A Concise Dictionary of Garden and General Horticulture and Cultivated Plants in North America.* New York: The Macmillan Company, 1947.

Ball, Jeff. *Rodale's Garden Problem Solver, Vegetables, Fruits and Herbs.* Emmaus, Pa.: Rodale Press, 1988.

Behler, John L. and F. Wayne King. *The Audubon Society Field Guide to North American Reptiles and Amphibians.* New York: Alfred A. Knopf, 1979.

Bolle, Kees, trans. *The Bhagavad Gita.* Berkeley: University of California Press, 1979.

Brickell, Christopher. *Pruning: Roses, Deciduous Shrubs, Evergreens, Hedges, Wall Shrubs, Fruit Bushes and Trees, Deciduous Trees.* New York: Simon and Schuster, 1979.

Buchanan, Carol. *Brother Crow, Sister Corn: Traditional American Indian Gardening.* Berkeley: Ten Speed Press, 1997.

Burton, Maurice. *Systematic Dictionary of Mammals of the World.* New York: Thomas Y. Cromwell Co., 1962.

Campbell, Joseph. *The Masks of God,* 4 vols.: *Primitive Mythology,* 1959; *Oriental Mythology,* 1962; *Occidental Mythology,* 1968; *Creative Mythology,* 1968. London: Penguin Books, 1962.

Carr, A., F. M. Bradley, and F. Marshall, eds. *Rodale's Chemical Free Yard and Garden.* Emmaus, Pa.: Rodale Press, 1991.

Coccannouer, Joseph A. *Weeds, Guardians of the Soil.* New York: Devin Adair, 1950.

Cogan, William Bryant. *Dirt; The Ecstatic Skin of the Earth.* New York: Riverhead Books, a Division of G.P. Putnam's Sons, 1995.

Colburn, Theo. *Our Stolen Future.* New York: Penguin Books USA, 1996.

Daubeny, Charles, M.D., F.R.S., M.R.I.A. Lectures on Roman Husbandry Delivered Before the University of Oxford: Comprehending Such an Account of the System of Agriculture, the Treatment of Domestic Animals, the Horticulture &C, Pursued in Ancient Times, As May Be Collected From the Scriptores Rei Rusticae, the Georgics of Virgil, and Other Classical Authorities With Notices of the Plants Mentioned in Columella and Virgil. University of Oxford, 1857.

Erickson, Jonathon. *Gardening for a Greener Planet: A Chemical Free Approach.* Blue Ridge Summit, Pa.: Tab Books, 1992.

Faulkner, Edward H. *Plowman's Folly.* New York: Grosset and Dunlap, 1943.

Fukuoka, Masanobu. *The One Straw Revolution.* Emmaus, Pa.: Rodale Press, 1978.

Gibbs, W. Wayt. "Neuroscience-Optical Illusions; Side Splitting." *Scientific American,* January 22, 2000.

Gimbutas, Marija. *The Civilization of the Goddess.* San Francisco: HarperSanFrancisco, 1991.

———. *The Language of the Goddess.* San Francisco: Harper and Row, 1989.

Gladwell, Malcolm. "The Mosquito Killer." *The New Yorker,* July 2, 2001.

Gleick, James. *Chaos.* New York: Penguin, 1997.

Graves, Robert. *The Greek Myths 2.* New York: Penguin Books, 1960.

Hill, John E., and James D. Smith. *Bats; A Natural History.* Dorset, England: Henry Ling, Ltd., 1986.

Hole, John W., Jr. *Human Anatomy and Physiology,* 5th ed. Dubuque, Iowa: Wm. C. Brown Publishers, 1990.

Hunter, Beatrice Trum. *Gardening Without Poisons.* Boston: Houghton Mifflin Co., 1971.

Hyams, Edward. *A History of Gardens and Gardening.* New York: Praeger Publishers, 1971.

Jashemski, Wilhelmina F. *The Gardens of Pompeii; Herculaneum and the Villas Destroyed by Vesuvius.* New Rochelle, N.Y.: Caratzas Brother, 1993.

Jayakar, Pupul. *The Earth Mother; Legends, Goddesses, and Ritual Arts of India.* San Francisco: Harper and Row, 1990.

Klawans, Harold L., M.D. *Toscanini's Fumble and Other Tales of Clinical Neurology.* New York: Bantam Books, 1988.

Klein, Hilary Dole, and Adrian M. Wenner. *Tiny Game Hunting: Environmentally Healthy Ways to Trap and Kill the Pests in Your House and Garden.* New York: Bantam Books, 1991.

Lansing, J. Stephen. *Priests and Programmers; Technologies of Power in the Engineered Landscape of Bali.* Princeton, N.J.: Princeton University Press, 1991.

————. *The Three Worlds of Bali.* New York: Praeger Scientific, 1983.

Larter, Raima, Robert Worth, and Brent Speelman. "Better Living Through Chaos," *The Economist,* September 18, 1999.

Manning, Lawrence. *The How and Why of Better Gardening.* Toronto, New York, London: Van Nostrand and Co., Inc., 1951.

Metcalf, C. L., and W. P. Flint. *Destructive and Useful Insects, Their Habits and Control,* 3rd ed. New York: McGraw Hill Book Company, 1951.

Milne, Lorus, and Margery Milne. *The Audubon Society Field Guide to North American Insects & Spiders.* New York: Alfred A. Knopf, 1980.

Mullen, Robert. *The Latter Day Saints: The Mormons Yesterday and Today.* Garden City, N.Y.: Doubleday, 1955.

National Center for Ecological Analysis and Synthesis, October 1999 workshop. Conservation Ecology (online journal).

Nikhilananda, Swami. *The Yogas and Other Works; Chosen and with a Biography by Swami Nikhilananda.* New York: Ramakrishna Vivekananda Center, 1953.

Nyad, Diana. *Other Shores.* New York: Random House, 1978.

Ordish, George. *The Constant Pest: A Short History of Pests and Their Control.* New York: Charles Schribner's Sons, 1976.

Pearlman, Barbara. *Gardener's Fitness; Weeding Out the Aches and Pains.* Dallas: Taylor Publishing, 1999.

Pfeiffer, Ehrenfried E. *Weeds and What They Tell.* Springfield, Ill.: Bio Dynamic Literature, 1974.

Philbrick, Helen, and John Philbrick. *The Bug Book.* Pownal, Vt.: Garden Way Publishing, 1974.

Physician's Desk Reference. Montvale, N.J.: Medical Economics Company, 1999.

Prabhavananda, Swami. *Bhagavad Gita,* trans. Christopher Isherwood. New York: Barnes and Noble Books, 1995.

Proceedings of the 1997 Great Lakes Endocrine Disrupters Symposium, U.S. Department of Environment Protection, Chicago, Illinois, July 14, 1997.

Rhoades, James, trans. *Virgil Great Books of the Western World.* Robert Maynard Hutchins, editor in chief. Chicago: Encyclopaedia Brittanica, 1952.

Sabuco, John J. *The Best of the Hardiest.* Flossmoor, Ill.: Good Earth Publishing Ltd., 1985.

Sackville-West, Vita. *Vita Sackville-West's Garden Book.* New York: Atheneum, 1967.

Sears, Paul B. *Deserts on the March.* Norman: University of Oklahoma Press, 1959.

Semple, Ellen Church. Paper read at a Joint Meeting of the Agricultural History Society with the American Historical Association, December 28, 1927.

Seymour, John. *The Self Sufficient Gardener.* New York: Dolphin Books, a division of Doubleday, 1980.

Sittig, Marshall. *The Handbook of Toxic and Hazardous Chemicals and Carcinogins,* 3rd ed. Westwood, N.J.: Noyes Data Corp., 1991.

Smith, Huston. *The Religions of Man.* New York: Harper and Row, 1958.

Stout, Ruth. *The No Work Garden Book.* Emmaus, Pa.: Rodale Press, 1971.

Strickland, Arvarh E. "The Strange Affair of the Boll Weevil: The Pest as Liberator." Eli Whitney's Cotton Gin, 1793–1993: A Symposium. Agricultural History Society, 1994.

Sunset Books, eds. *Sunset New Western Garden Book.* Menlo Park, Calif.: Lane Publishing Co., 1979.

Suzuki, Daisetz T. *Essays in Zen Buddhism,* 1st series. London: Rider and Co., 1949.

———. *Zen and Japanese Culture.* New York: MJF Books, published by arrangement with Princeton University Press, 1959.

Svobida, Lawrence. *An Empire of Dust.* Caldwell, Idaho: The Caxton Printers, 1940.

Swain, Ralph B., Ph.D. *The Insect Guide.* Garden City, N.Y.: The Country Life Press, 1948.

Technological Development and Demonstration. European Union's Fifth Programme for Research. European Commission. ENERGIE Publication.

Tenner, Edward, Ph.D. *Why Things Bite Back: Technology and the Revenge of Unintended Consequences.* New York: Alfred A. Knopf, 1996.

Thich Nhat Hanh. *Old Path White Clouds.* Berkeley: Parallax Press, 1991.

Tuttle, Merlin D. *America's Neighborhood Bats.* Austin: University of Texas Press, 1988.

Twain, Mark. *Letters from the Earth,* ed. Bernarad De Voto. New York: Perennial Library Harper and Row, 1962.

U.S. Department of Agriculture. *Common Weeds of the United States.* New York: Dover Publications, 1971.

U.S. Geological Survey. *Introduction to the Malformed Amphibian Issue.* Washington, D.C.: U.S. Department of the Interior, January 15, 2002.

Walker, Evan Harris, Ph.D. *The Physics of Consciousness.* New York: Perseus Publishing, a division of HarperCollins, 2000.

Whitaker, John O., Jr. *The Audubon Society Field Guide to North American Mammals.* New York: Alfred A. Knopf, 1980.

White, E. B. *One Man's Meat.* New York: Harper and Row, 1982.

White, Katherine. *Onward and Upward in the Garden,* ed. E. B. White. New York: Farrar, Straus & Giroux, 1979.

Wild Animals of North America. Washington, D.C.: National Geographic Society, 1987.

Wright, Michael, ed. *The Complete Book of Gardening.* New York Warner Books, 1980.

Yepson, Roger B., Jr., ed. *Organic Plant Protection.* Emmaus, Pa.: Rodale Press, 1976.

Some Useful Periodicals

House and Garden. Conde Nast Publications, Inc., Conde Nast Building, 4 Times Square, New York, NY 10036.

The Lancet (United Kingdom Medical Journal). The Lancet Publishing Group, 650 Avenue of the Americas, New York, NY 10011.

OG (Organic Gardening). Rodale, Inc., 33 E. Minor Street, Emmaus, PA 18098.

Pomona, member written quarterly journal of North American Fruit Explorers. Subscription information: http://www.nafex.org

Science News. Science Service, Washington, D.C.

Scientific American. 415 Madison Avenue, New York, NY 10017-1111.

ACKNOWLEDGMENTS

*I would like to thank the following people whose help
and support made this book possible:*

My husband, Walter, whose steadying influence,
silliness, and handyman's skills make life worth living, as well
as more comfortable.

Dmitri and Ariadne Sandbeck, for research and editorial
assistance and modeling services.

Grace Miller and Eleanor Nichol, for their wise
and generous friendship.

Susie Newman, Carolyn Olson, Tim Kaiser, Charlie
and Jim Nichol, Al, Lynda, Joseph and Freddie Parella,
Arna Rennan—gardening friends and inspirations.

Rosie Korzeniowski, O.T.R., body mechanics consultant
and supermodel.

Frank and Anna Sjodin, for modeling services.

Liz Sarabia, for nursery and greenhouse information.

New neighbors John, Tide, Ben, and Kathy Pearson, for
helping us adjust to country life, and for feeding us so well!

Al Hagen, P.T., exercise consultant.
Theresa Koenig and Ann Klefstad, for invaluable help
with the manuscript.

Dan Klun, for information on asphalt recycling.

My agent, Janis Donnaud, for her lightheartedness and
encouragement.

The diligent and heroic research librarians at the
Duluth Public Library.

Thank you all!

INDEX